Little Free Libraries & Tiny Sheds

Little Free Libraries & Tiny Sheds

12
MINIATURE STRUCTURES
YOU CAN BUILD

PHILIP SCHMIDT &
LITTLE FREE LIBRARY

LITTLE FREE LIBRARY.ORG®
TAKE A BOOK · SHARE A BOOK

COOL
SPRINGS
PRESS

CONTENTS

Foreword

Whoever said "from small things, great things grow" would have loved Little Free Libraries.

At the Little Free Library nonprofit organization, where I serve as founder and executive director, we have a simple but powerful mission: to inspire a love of reading, build community, and spark creativity by fostering neighborhood book exchanges around the world.

At a Little Free Library book-sharing station, folks of any age, background, or income bracket can stop and find a book to take home or donate a book for someone else to discover. At the same time, they can strike up a conversation with a stranger, get to know their neighbors, and feel more deeply connected to their community.

When it comes to literacy and community, there is certainly work to be done. In low-income neighborhoods in the United States, there is only one book for every three hundred children. And research shows that one-third of us have never met our neighbors.

In 2009, when I built the first Little Free Library, I wasn't expecting to launch a global literacy and community movement. I built the first Little Free Library as a memorial to my mother, who was a lifelong reader and educator and whose memory I wanted to keep alive. But the reaction my neighbors had to the book-sharing box was beautiful: they stopped to talk, they lingered, they shared stories, they connected with each other—and of course they shared books too. I knew then that I wanted to inspire literacy and community through a Little Free Library Sharing Network.

In 2010, I was trying to find support for the Little Free Library concept. We had only sold three or four libraries in six months—pretty dismal results. As I was thinking about throwing in the towel, I heard a piece on National Public Radio about Martin Luther King Jr. When asked, "What would you do if you were going to die tomorrow?" he said he would plant a seed, because a seed can grow, change, and produce a better future.

That was the example I wanted to follow: to plant seeds of literacy and community. So we gave away thirty Little Free Libraries. Bit by bit, more libraries started to sprout, the media and public started to support us, and the movement started to grow.

Today, there are more than 75,000 Little Free Libraries around the world, in all fifty states and eighty-five countries, sharing tens of millions of books each year.

These small book-sharing boxes can have a big impact on a community. We have heard time and time again that when someone starts a Little Free Library, they meet more neighbors in a week than they've met in the last ten years. We have also seen how access to books can change a life: from a person who is homeless finding a much-needed book to read, to a reluctant elementary-age reader who grows to love books because of a Little Free Library's magic.

But even now, we still have miles to go. We're helping bring more Little Free Libraries full of books to lower-income neighborhoods through our Impact Library Program. We're creating ways for police officers and families to connect via our Kids, Community & Cops Program. And we're connecting reading and community service through our Action Book Club. (Visit www.littlefreelibrary.org to join!)

We're delighted that you're reading this book and are interested in starting a Little Free Library in your neighborhood. Whether it is at your home, school, park, church, or business, your Little Free Library will stand as a signpost of kindness and connection in your community.

Pictured above is Todd Bol's very first Little Free Library.

I've been asked many times what the secret is behind the success of the Little Free Library movement, and the answer is: It's you! The most important pieces of the Little Free Library puzzle are the people behind each Little Free Library.

The Little Free Library Sharing Network empowers individuals to become community heroes who use their libraries in many ways. Some stewards place an emphasis on children's books, to keep kids reading all year long. Some host a seed exchange inside the sharing box so neighbors can trade flower and vegetable seeds. Still others host Little Free Pantries that offer nonperishable food and toiletry items for neighbors in need. Each library comes to reflect what the community needs most.

We're thrilled to welcome you to the Little Free Library Sharing Network, and we invite you to explore how a Little Free Library can benefit your community. With Little Free Libraries, we are coming together, we are connecting, and we are reading. And these small seeds of literacy and community keep growing and growing.

TODD H. BOL

PUBLISHER'S NOTE: Todd Bol passed away in October 2018 shortly after writing this foreword and being diagnosed with pancreatic cancer. He was heartened by the growing network of Little Free Library stewards around the world working to build stronger, more-connected communities.

Introduction

LET'S GET SMALL

In recent years, "tiny" has become something of a buzzword among home enthusiasts, from the sawdust-in-their-hair DIY folks to the dreamy-eyed crowd that pores over glossy magazines and schedules their evenings around twenty-four-hour cable networks that explore every nook and cranny of home ownership. The appeal should come as little surprise: tiny homes promote sustainability, offer possible solutions to a growing paucity of affordable housing, suggest a pathway to simplifying cluttered modern lives, and (let's face it) are just cool.

But aside from these popular and cozy habitable homes, what about the *really* tiny structures we also see with increasing frequency, those that are sprouting up on urban lawns and along rural roadsides, in schoolyards and public parks, from coast to coast? Many, if not most, of these structures serve as lending libraries, a movement begun by Todd H. Bol, founder of the Little Free Library organization (see Foreword). Their designs are limited only by the imaginations and resources of their owners. These libraries can take the form of simple-yet-sturdy plywood boxes, or they can be complex mimetic endeavors suggesting everything from seventeenth-century farmhouses with scale-sized clapboard siding to midcentury teardrop campers.

Somewhere along the way, though, civic-minded individuals adapted the Little Free Library concept. Now, in addition to housing paperbacks and CDs, we can find tiny structures that serve as seed libraries in community gardens or as pantries for those in need. Others provide handy backyard tool storage for gardeners and urban farmers (see pages 69–73 and 129–135). Like all good ideas, the concept has been adapted and thus grown beyond its original intention. What began as an effort to foster community togetherness through sharing books has spurred the rise of tiny (usually) pole-mounted structures serving numerous ends.

Inside this book you will find instructions for twelve tiny structures, including a garden box and garden shed (above). While the other ten plans are ostensibly libraries (including one that recreates Bol's first-ever Little Free Library), how you use the finished structures is up to you. Elsewhere in the book are instructions and advice for everything you need to know about building, mounting, maintaining, and even registering your Little Free Library, and then spreading the word about your new sharing box.

This book is your entrée to the growing world of little libraries and tiny sheds. Whether you intend to build a structure to create a gathering place on your block or just to save yourself a trip from your garden to your garage, we hope you'll find it useful and instructional.

So sit back and let's get started. Little libraries and tiny sheds may be small in stature, but they're big on possibilities.

—COOL SPRINGS PRESS

Planning & Design

1

Now that you're getting serious about having a little structure of your very own, what do you want yours to be? What shape will it have? How big will it be? Where will it go? And most importantly, what will it do? These and other essential planning questions will help you get from the drawing board to a useful, lovable, tiny building with as little trouble as possible. And there's no reason to rush through the process—dreaming and planning are half the fun.

The first question to address is "What will your structure do?" Is it intended for sharing with neighbors, donating useful items, or simply storing stuff you'd like to keep at hand? Maybe it does more than one thing, or maybe the initial use will evolve into other uses. (Just because it's tiny doesn't mean it's not versatile.) The primary purpose, or purposes, of the structure will say a lot about what it should look like, where it should live, and how it should be built.

Where your structure lives is an important consideration that may involve decision makers outside your household—namely, those at city hall or your homeowners association (HOA). While restrictions are not very common, some cities and HOAs have rules about (or against) little structures intended for public sharing, and some may impose requirements on anything you put in your front yard. It's best to check with the powers that be before taking your project to the drawing board.

For some people, the biggest question may be the *how*: how will you turn your vision into reality? There are many options. You can buy a finished little building, and even an assembled post mount, ready to install. At the other end of the spectrum, you might design a totally custom project and build it all from scratch. Somewhere in the

A structure mounted lower than its companion box creates a special place for young visitors in Limerick, Ireland.

middle, a lot of tiny-structure builders choose to upcycle a found or salvaged item, creating something that's both unique and resource-efficient.

In this chapter, you'll learn about all these options and considerations, as well as some tips and ideas for decorating and outfitting your structure to make it truly yours. Want to make it kid-friendly? Or maybe dog-friendly? How about lighting it up with a built-in night-light?

WHAT WILL YOUR STRUCTURE DO?

Planning starts here because a structure's purpose is the primary guide behind most aspects of its design. You might approach this by asking a related question: what do you want to share or store? The items housed in your building dictate its size and sometimes its shape and interior layout.

For example, if you want to share books, you'll need plenty of space for standard-size books, and perhaps some extra room for a shelf or two (see Sizing for Books on page 13). If you'd like your structure to promote sharing of other items—like seeds or tools or dog toys—you might include special shelves or compartments designed for these items.

Multiple shelves not only increase storage space but also make items more accessible to both kids and adults. One fun way to serve the littlest kids is to include a separate mini structure that mounts below the main structure. The same idea can be used to create a self-serve compartment for dogs.

A simple method to determine how much space you might need as well as how to lay out the interior of your structure is to gather some representative items and measure them—together and individually. If you want the flexibility to store tall items when necessary, you can plan for adjustable shelves that can be moved or removed as needed.

IDEAS FOR ALL TYPES OF TINY STRUCTURES

Sharing books is just one way to use tiny structures. They're also great for exchanging other things, for donating goods, or even for personal storage in nonpublic locations. Here are a few ideas for different uses (the ideas are free for the taking, so don't hesitate to borrow, share, give away, or build on any of them):

- Gardeners' exchange—tools, seeds, homegrown foods, growing tips
- Tool booth—go-to yard and garden tools (see page 129)
- Homeowners' depot—home repair and remodeling tools, DIY books, building materials, hardware
- CD swap—music, movies, video games
- Kitchen pantry—kitchen tools, recipes, cookbooks, dry goods, food magazines
- Clothes and equipment closet—hand-me-down clothes for babies, kids, or adults; outgrown cleats and helmets; unused balls, bats, and racquets
- Board game library—for finding or sharing family favorites
- Give box—food, clothing, and other essentials for the needy

SIZING FOR BOOKS

Books come in all shapes and sizes (thankfully), but most are no taller than 12″ and no wider than 11″. Standard bookshelves tend to be around 12″ tall and 11″ to 12″ deep. Large coffee-table books and art books are notable exceptions but seldom are wider than 12″, allowing them to fit on a shelf when laid flat.

When planning a structure for sharing books, make sure the usable interior space is at least 12″ high, 12″ deep, and 12″ wide. That's a pretty small lending library, so you might go bigger than that. If you go high enough, you can accommodate a second shelf, even if it's a short shelf area (great for small paperbacks and children's board books) above a standard 12″-high shelf, or a compartment below.

Make sure your library has plenty of usable interior space—including a second shelf, if possible, and even compartments for smaller paperback series.

DESIGNING FOR VISITORS

Structures intended for community lending or sharing present some special considerations. Since the object is to attract lots of visitors for an active and lively exchange, the structure should be both inviting and user-friendly. It should also be designed to handle all those visitors and their *handling* of the structure.

Mounting: *Make sure your structure is secure and, in most cases, off the ground.* Whether it's parked next to the sidewalk in front of your house or on community property or in another public place, structures designed for sharing tend to work best when mounted on a post, fence, tree, or other handy permanent support. Structures off the ground get noticed and are easy to work around with snow shovels and the like. They're also securely anchored to the ground so they can't be tipped over (and are less likely to wander off in the night).

Visibility: *Make sure visitors can see your structure.* Choose a location that will be noticeable to passersby, and think about design features that are inviting. For example, a see-through door provides an instant glimpse of what's inside, which can be much more meaningful than a sign. When visitors are exploring the contents up close, a brightly painted interior eliminates shadows and dark corners in the back of the structure.

Accessibility: *Make sure visitors can get to your structure.* Accessibility is related to mounting (where and how high you install your structure) and to visibility (making it noticeable), but it also incorporates usability factors: Is it a nice place to stop and browse the collection? Can everyone get to it easily? Can it be seen at night? See page 23 for some easy ways to add lighting.

Signage: *Let visitors know what your structure is about.* Don't assume everyone will understand how to use your exchange, or even that they're familiar with Little Free Libraries. Include a sign (or lettering) with basic instructions for using the exchange. A few popular examples:

- "Take a Book, Share a Book"
- "Give What You Can, Take What You Need"
- "Need Something? Take Something. Have Something? Leave Something."
- "Take One, Leave One"
- "Help Another, Help Yourself"
- "Free (fill in the blank)"

You can also include notes suggesting a theme for your exchange:
- "Seed Exchange"
- "Books about Animals"
- "Field Guides"

Visibility and accessibility are critical when placing your library. And what's more visible and accessible than a low garden wall outside a London rowhouse?

Door Features: *Design your door for the masses.* Provide means for keeping the door closed, whether it's a turn-button latch, an antique gate handle, or a magnetic catch. If you find that your door is left open even though it has a latch, consider installing self-closing hinges. Other essential door features include acrylic glazing instead of glass (for safety; see Glazing on page 28) and a design that keeps out rain and snow (see Mother Nature on page 29).

Amenities: *Consider user experience.* Successful exchanges not only attract new visitors; they also turn first-time visitors into regulars. Here are a few ideas for built-in features that will keep 'em coming back (also see Tips for a Lively Collection on page 154):

- Seating area(s)
- Dog-leash hook
- Low shelf or mini structure for tiny visitors (of all species)
- Compartment for bookmarks, community fliers, comment or request cards, and so on
- Tethered bike tools
- Lights (see Lighting on page 23)

LOCATION, PERMISSION & OTHER CONSIDERATIONS

Finding the best location, getting permission, and addressing concerns about public use (and related problems such as vandalism) are primary considerations for structures intended for community sharing. If you're building a structure for private use in your backyard, you might not need a go-ahead from anyone besides other household members. Just be aware that if your city considers your structure to be an "accessory building," it may be subject to setback rules and other zoning restrictions. Setbacks prohibit permanent structures within a given distance from your property line. For

Place your structure out of the way of pedestrians, cyclists, lawn mowers, and snow plows. Give them space!

example, a city may not allow structures within 5 feet of a property line at the sides or rear of a lot, or within 20 or more feet from the front curb or street.

CHOOSING A LOCATION

If your structure is set up for neighborhood or community exchange, you want others to feel as though the structure belongs to them, not just you. After all, it's your gift to the neighborhood. Make sure it's easy to find, easy to see from the street or sidewalk, and easy to reach. It also helps if you can see the structure from a nearby window in your house.

The little building is its own best advertising, especially if people driving by can see it and stop without blocking traffic. If possible, try to have it within reach of streetlights or give it its own lighting.

If you install your structure in front of your home, place it on your property near the sidewalk, not on the boulevard between the sidewalk and the street.

To install your structure on public property, be sure to get the proper permission. You may need to check with park boards, school administrators, business owners, or other decision makers.

GOVERNING AUTHORITIES

Many people wonder why governments have so many policies, rules, and regulations, or why it seems that they make it so hard to do something nice. The same might be said of HOAs. Regardless of the name or type of authority, they're all governing bodies that have similar concerns, such as:

- Liability and safety
- Right of way—both legal and actual—for snowplows, bicyclists, walkers, and cars and other vehicles
- Physical maintenance in case of damage or normal wear and tear
- Appropriateness for the general public (children and adults)

In addition, a parks administrator or streets engineer might ask who will be responsible for both the structure and its contents over the long term. If an organization or individual is the key contact, for example, what should the government agency do when that person is no longer willing or able to be the caretaker of the structure?

In short, government officials want to minimize the administrative burden while trying to satisfy various public wishes. And the bigger the city, the more rigorous the zoning laws can be. Small-town governments tend to have more flexibility.

If your hope is to install a community structure, find out whose regulations and rules might apply. Confirm that your plans fall within those regulations. If they don't, consider how you can make it as easy as possible to do what you want anyway. Here are some options:

- Avoid the problem entirely by putting your structure *near* public land but not *on* it—for example, across the street or nearby, on property that belongs to someone who is willing (even eager) to have it there.
- Talk to the person in charge of enforcing or managing compliance with the regulations. Ask for his or her advice rather than permission. Explain how the exchange will belong to everyone and should cause no major problems. Take a picture of the spot you'd like to use, or invite the official to show you a better place. Ask what you need to do to comply. It might be easier than you think.
- Fill out and submit the required applications or permit forms.
- Seek a variance in the zoning rules if absolutely necessary. Provide evidence that your project (an exchange provided for the neighborhood, not just for one family) deserves it.
- Suggest that the government, HOA, or co-op board obtain the structure, and that you or your group work with them to support and maintain it.
- Be nice. If things don't work out exactly as you would like, ask something like "Is there any other way I can locate my structure in this area or nearby? Where do you (the official) think might be a good place?"

As an example of how a city parks department might handle these matters, here are the basic proposal requirements from the city of Madison, Wisconsin, to request a park modification such as a library or other exchange:

1. Detailed description of the project
2. Exact location in the park (with a map, if possible)
3. Maintenance and upkeep plan
4. Any alterations or impacts to the park, if applicable
5. Budget
6. Timeline for implementation

VANDALISM

The question of vandalism is a natural one. You might wonder, "Who would damage a free library or a neighborhood give box?" Well, the same kind of person who might set off firecrackers in mailboxes. Thrill seekers. Kids in groups, for example. Drunk people.

The next natural question is, what might keep them from doing that? The answer lies in thinking like a mischief maker. The more he believes that he might be caught, the less likely he is to do the damage. When planning where your exchange will be, try answering these questions from a vandal's point of view:

PRETTY PLEASE!

Whether you're still seeking approval or already have permission, here are few ideas to help make your structure even more popular:

- Mount it on a wall or fence, or next to a garden.
- Incorporate it into a rest stop or shelter, or next to an existing bench.
- Plant flowers or other landscaping around it.
- Add a bench so visitors can sit and spend some time with items they find in your exchange.
- Keep it clean, inside and out.

- "Will someone see me?" If the structure is in your front yard, keep your front light on or have it near a streetlight. Put it where passing traffic can see it.
- "Will it be easy to break or take?" If it has glass in it, yes. Plexiglas can be easily broken too, but you can replace it. If your structure has artwork or hardware that can be removed, you are tempting fate.
- "Can I break off a piece of the structure?" Anything that sticks out can be awfully tempting to someone inclined toward vandalism or rushes of youthful energy.
- "Does anybody really care?" If the structure is surrounded by weeds and trash, or is not well maintained, it's more likely to be damaged. If it's in the front yard of a beloved, friendly neighbor, it's more likely to be safe.

Let anyone who lives near the exchange know that it has an owner with a name who cares about it. Friends, family, and neighbors who know one another will cherish and protect the exchange more than strangers will. Anything that implies that this little building belongs to the community, especially people with names and faces, can reinforce the idea that damaging it hurts someone.

Worried about "bad kids"? Why not invite them into the circle of protectors? Tell them about the exchange and how it works. Give them books or other shared items. Make them feel important.

Leave a handwritten note or a sign that says something like "Thank you for protecting and loving our library!" Such a message can show that people do care and that watching out for this little property is the neighborhood norm.

WHAT TO DO IF YOUR STRUCTURE IS VANDALIZED

Repair it as soon as possible. Remind yourself to believe in the goodness of the vast majority of people. If you think it will help, move the structure to a less risky location.

Let it be known in a positive way that a precious neighborhood resource has been damaged. Notify the community through neighborhood chat rooms or through the Little Free Library Facebook group. It's not uncommon for stories of vandalism or damage to turn into tales of inspiration—where wounded exchanges were mysteriously repaired or replaced, or communities found donors to rebuild them.

Any or all of the ideas above are probably more effective than yelling at or fighting with roaming bands of troublemakers. Don't challenge those who did the damage to do it again by threatening or confronting them. If you do, everybody loses.

BUY, FIND, ASSEMBLE, OR BUILD YOUR OWN?

Now that you know you want a little building, and you maybe even have a good idea about where you'll put it, you have several options. But before you make up your mind, take a look at the building projects on pages 49–135 to get an idea of what goes into a tiny structure, including tools, materials, design, and construction steps. This will give you a sense of what's involved in building your own structure, as well as the value of a prebuilt structure.

BUYING A PREBUILT STRUCTURE

The easiest option is to buy a tiny building that's preassembled, prepainted, and ready to install. The building can cost $300 or more, plus (in many cases) another $50 to $80 for shipping. A prebuilt post base might cost $65 or more and about the same amount for additional shipping.

Those numbers may give you a bit of sticker shock, but if you're not someone who relishes the idea of spending a weekend in your garage (and driving around town for supplies), or if you don't even have a garage or a suitable workspace, a premade building can be an excellent value. You can also reduce your cost by getting an unfinished building and finding a supplier that offers free shipping. If you're up for a small construction project, you can save more by building your own post base (see Building a Wood Post Base on page 138).

Prebuilt structures are sold by the Little Free Library organization via their website and Amazon. Or you can work with a local builder to create your Little Free Library masterpiece and then register it (see page 156).

ASSEMBLING A KIT

If you're drawn to the time savings and convenience of a prebuilt structure but prefer a bit more of a hands-on experience, you can purchase a kit from the Little Free Library organization. Kits are flat-packed and typically consist of four complete walls, a floor (base), and a roof. The door and wall trim may be installed already. Kits also include screws, nails, and any other required fasteners and hardware. You must supply wood glue and paint or another type of exterior finish.

Assembling a kit requires a drill-driver (for driving screws), a hammer, and, if desired, a nail set (see Screwing and Nailing in Wood on page 33). The basic assembly may take only about an

Kits include all the parts you need and often have predrilled holes for nails and screws so you can't miss the wood no matter how unhandy you are. This is Little Free Library's "Reader's Classic" model, available from their website.

hour, then the structure is ready for finishing (which takes about a day, including drying time). You can also prefinish most of the parts before assembling. The One-Story Shed Kit project on pages 47–51 shows you the basic steps of assembling a kit structure.

FINDING A SUITABLE BUILDING

There are a few ways you might find a little structure. You might own or come across an existing structure—most likely a container of some kind—that can be adapted easily into a tiny building. It has to be watertight and weather-resistant and have a secure door to keep out rain. You might be surprised at what meets these criteria: a mini fridge; an outdoor storage bench; an old newspaper dispenser (a real find for this purpose); a toolbox, mailbox, or breadbox; and so on.

Whatever it is, it must be safe: no sharp metal or protruding screws, no glass, no easy way for little fingers to get hurt, no toxic refrigerants (have that mini fridge decommissioned by a certified technician).

Repurposing an existing structure is another possibility for creating your own Little Free Library. It just needs to be watertight with a secure door to keep out the elements.

Another source of free or found structures might be an organization that donates structures or builds them for communities and individuals, such as:

- Girl Scout or Boy Scout troops
- Local carpenters and artists
- Schools, churches, and community centers
- Rotary, 4-H, Kiwanis, and Lions clubs
- Little Free Library

Contact these or other local organizations to learn about getting help with setting up a library or other type of exchange in your community.

BUILDING YOUR OWN

If you like the idea of building a little structure from scratch but carpentry is a real stretch on your résumé, don't feel intimidated. Many of the tens of thousands of tiny libraries and other exchanges around the world were built by ordinary people just like you. It can be enormously satisfying to create a little structure with your own hands, whether you're following plans with measured drawings like those found in this book or dreaming up your own design.

IDEAS FOR ADDING CURB APPEAL

Buttons, bicycle gears, bottle caps, Mardi Gras beads, hockey sticks, twigs, spiral staircases, electric guitars, herb gardens, robot arms, and Darth Vader heads. What do these things have in common? They've all been used to decorate tiny structures. When it comes to dolling up your doll-size building, anything goes. So have fun!

Creative decorating is one of the best ways to get your structure noticed and to share your interests (be they hobbies or favorite books or characters) with the community. Another way to add appeal and attract first-time and repeat visitors is to include user-friendly amenities. A few of the most popular are a guest book, a dog-leash hook, and automatic lighting. Here are some tips for adding these simple upgrades to your structure.

GUEST BOOK

A guest book gives visitors a place to share notes, requests, thank-yous, or just an everyday hello. It's also a great way for caretakers to gauge how many visitors are stopping by and perhaps to learn what they're interested in.

A small, spiral-bound notebook with hard covers makes a handy and easy-to-use guest book. To keep things tidy and prevent the guest book from falling to the ground or getting mixed up with the other contents, secure it with a strong string or cord fastened to the side of the structure. Better yet, connect it to a retracting keychain or lanyard anchored at the top of one of the walls. Be sure to include a pen or pencil, also on a tether or attached to the guest book.

Some charitable organizations and volunteer groups purchase and assemble kits to provide free exchanges to underserved communities.

DOG-LEASH HOOK

Give visitors a handy place to park their pooch. All it takes is a big eye lag (a lag screw with a closed loop at one end) and a carabiner. The eye lag screws into the structure's mounting

ABOVE AND RIGHT:
Your options for
decorating and adding
curb appeal to your
library are limitless.
Have fun!

post or other nearby solid-wood structure. Dog walkers clip the handle of their leash onto the carabiner, which has a spring-loaded gate to keep the leash secure.

Make sure to use a carabiner that's load-rated for several hundred pounds and is made with rustproof materials. There are plenty of carabiner keychains and other flimsy knockoffs that might not be strong enough for this application. Also make sure to use a heavy-duty ⅜-inch or larger diameter eye lag made of hot-dipped galvanized steel or stainless steel. It should go at least 3 inches into the center of the wood post. Start the lag in the pilot hole by tapping it a few times with a hammer, then turning the screw with pliers or an adjustable wrench. Once the threads have grabbed the wood, you can stick one handle of a pair of pliers or a long screwdriver into the eye to turn the screw.

LIGHTING

Lights aren't just charming and inviting; they also send the message that your structure is always open for business. Solar lights are ideal because they power themselves, and most include a photocell (light sensor) that automatically turns on the lights at sundown and turns them off at sunrise. You can also use battery-powered lights that work on a timer or, for the electrically inclined, a door button.

Adding a solar light can be as simple as mounting the light's solar panel to the roof of the structure and running a wire into the light inside. This requires a unit with a separate solar panel and light, which is handy for interior lighting.

A self-contained solar landscape light or deck light works well for exterior lighting. You can mount a path fixture to shine like a beacon from the structure's roof. A deck light (or step light) works well for lighting a building's facade.

These solar lights typically contain a small solar panel, an internal rechargeable battery (to store solar-generated power during daylight hours), and a low-wattage LED light bulb. You can modify most fixtures as long as you keep these parts connected. For example, a solar path light with a metal post will work just as well without the post. Tinker around with one—they cost only a few bucks—to see how you can customize it to suit your structure.

TOP: An interior light is like a welcoming **OPEN** sign, and because it's solar, it stays on all night and recharges itself during the day. **A lightly stained or painted interior also helps eliminate shadows and dark corners. MIDDLE: A** length of gardener's twine or a retractable tether like those used for security passes (shown here) works well for attaching a guest book to your library. **BOTTOM:** Fasten your guestbook in a visible location and tether it to keep it from getting lost.

Building Basics

If you're an experienced builder, this chapter might not teach you anything new, but you might find some helpful tips and reminders. For novice builders, the information here will help ensure your little structure is ready to stand up to the weather and lots of use, whether you intend to follow one of the project plans in Chapter 3 or branch out with a custom design.

After this quick primer on building basics, you'll be ready to move on to the fun part: actually building something.

GOOD MATERIALS FOR LITTLE STRUCTURES

When it comes to choosing construction materials, all outdoor structures are essentially the same, whether they're houses for people, sheds for lawnmowers, or tiny buildings for books. Anything exposed to the weather must be suitable for outdoors, and this includes being painted or otherwise protected from water and sunlight.

WOOD MATERIALS

For the basic structure, you don't have to sweat your choice of wood too much, because you'll be slathering it with a good coating of paint (or other finish). Any solid wood or plywood will do. You can use marine plywood, which is made with waterproof glue, or exterior plywood (the only grade of standard plywood designed for long-term weather exposure), but they aren't necessary. Pressure-treated (PT) lumber, which is chemically treated for rot-resistance, is recommended for the post or any parts that contact the ground, but it's not necessary for the structure. Also, you might not want the wood's chemicals mingling with your structure's contents.

As for solid wood, any regular wood species is suitable. Redwood and cedar are worth the extra cost only if you desire their look. Most standard grades of cedar and redwood aren't as rot-resistant as their reputation suggests, and all of them weather just like pine and other common softwoods. But if you give redwood or cedar a nice stain or clear protective finish, they can be really beautiful.

Wood composites like medium-density fiberboard (MDF) and particleboard are nice and smooth when you buy them, and they're cheap and easy to work with, but they're also prone to water damage. If real wood gets wet, it simply starts to weather; if MDF or particleboard gets wet, it bubbles and swells up. Sometimes composites are unavoidable, as they're commonly used for cabinet boxes and prefab wood accents (see the Kitchen Cabinet Upcycle on page 121). In this case, just be sure to seal the wood thoroughly—especially the edges—with paint or caulk.

The strongest and least expensive type of wood for posts and foundations is PT lumber. Make sure it's rated for ground contact if it will be buried or will sit on the ground. PT lumber isn't the best-looking wood out there, but it can be painted or stained, or left unfinished to weather to a rough gray that looks pretty much like weathered cedar.

FASTENERS AND HARDWARE

All metal materials on your structure should be made for outdoor exposure. On the inside of the structure, where rain and snow may never reach, you might get away with standard metal parts, but even high humidity can rust unprotected metal, and screws and nail heads can bleed rust even if they're painted. It's best to stick with corrosion-resistant materials for all metal parts. Common options include:

BELOW LEFT: Plywood is ideal for the sides, top, and bottom of the box structures, and it works well for custom doors. You can use 1/2"-, 5/8"-, or 3/4"-thick material for box parts; 3/4" is best for doors. **BELOW RIGHT TOP:** Look on the grade stamp of pressure-treated lumber to determine whether it's suitable for ground contact or above-ground use (pictured). **BELOW RIGHT BOTTOM:** Solid lumber, such as I × I, I × 2, I × 3, or wider boards, is good for trim and other parts with exposed edges. A solid-wood edge doesn't have voids and paints or stains better than the layered edge of plywood.

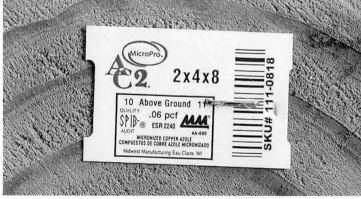

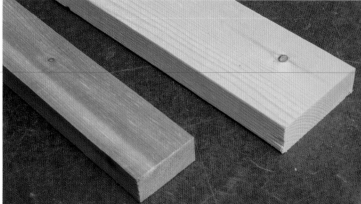

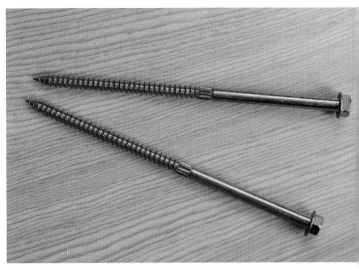

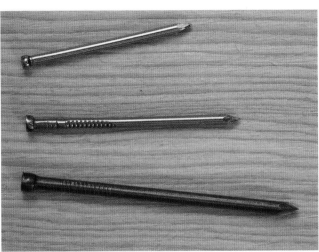

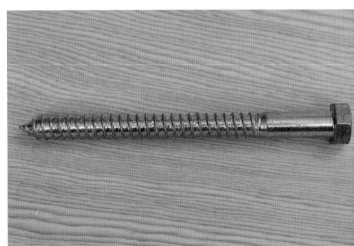

- Galvanized steel
- Aluminum
- Stainless steel
- Copper
- Solid brass (not brass finish)
- Coated steel (as in deck screws)

Galvanized steel is the most common and least expensive fastener and hardware material and is perfectly acceptable for this application. Hot-dipped galvanized (HDG) fasteners are generally more corrosion-resistant than smooth electroplated or simply zinc-coated fasteners. All are suitable for most applications, but only HDG is rated for PT lumber.

The common alternative to galvanized steel is stainless steel, the Superman of outdoor hardware materials. It's stronger than all the other metals and more corrosion-resistant than galvanized and other coated materials. It's generally overkill for most tiny structures, but you might splurge on it if you live in a coastal area and really want to avoid rust (in which case you should use grade

ABOVE LEFT: Deck screws and galvanized wood screws are used for structural connections, like joining box parts. Deck screws are specially coated for corrosion resistance and have coarse threads that bite into plywood or softwood lumber. **ABOVE RIGHT:** Timber screws are high-strength structural screws often used in place of lag screws. They usually have a hex head and can be driven with a drill and driver bit. **ABOVE BOTTOM LEFT:** Use exterior-rated finish nails to install wood trim and other decorative elements. They have small heads that are less noticeable than standard nail heads. **ABOVE BOTTOM RIGHT:** Screws that will go into pressure-treated posts or boards should be **HDG**, stainless steel, or otherwise rated for pressure-treated lumber.

316 stainless steel). Stainless fasteners are also suitable for PT lumber.

Glue is another type of fastener commonly used on tiny structures. There are standard wood glues and waterproof wood glues. You can probably guess which type is better for outdoor projects. If you need to join wood to metal, plastic, or other nonwood parts, use polyurethane glue (such as Gorilla Glue) or a two-part epoxy.

GLAZING

Glazing is just a fancy word for window material. For this application, the only thing that makes sense is plastic, such as acrylic or polycarbonate. Glass is simply too risky. The best-known acrylic glazing is Plexiglas; the best-known polycarbonate is Lexan. Both are easy to cut and drill and are plenty tough enough for the job. Polycarbonate is much stronger and somewhat more scratch-resistant than acrylic, but it's also much more expensive.

Scratches are the primary drawback of plastic glazing. Over the years, the tiny scratches and fissures will make the window cloudy, but it's easy enough to replace with a fresh piece. See Cutting and Drilling Plastic Glazing on page 35.

TOP: Make sure the metal materials on your structure were made for outdoor use. ABOVE: Plastic glazing gets scratched over time but is much safer than glass and can withstand a fair amount of abuse.

ROOFING

The roof's job is to take one for the team, day in and day out. It gets hit with most of the rain and snow and more than its share of the sun exposure. You can use almost anything for a roof material, as long as it keeps out water. Just bear in mind that a painted roof or any material that's not normally used outdoors might require more frequent upkeep than a standard roofing material.

All standard roofing materials—shingles, metal roofing, wood shakes, and so on—work well and can be cut down to the scale of the little structure. You can also improvise with outdoor-ready materials like galvanized or aluminum sheet metal. Traditional cedar or redwood lap siding makes an attractive roof, if you happen to have some on hand. It's best to finish this with an oil stain (to keep the wood from drying out) rather than paint.

Whatever material you use, make sure there's a way for water to drain by itself and drip to the ground and not on the walls of the structure (see Ready for Rain down below for tips on dealing with water). Also make sure that a flat roof isn't flat—it must have at least a little bit of slope to shed water. Seal any roof seams with a good silicone caulk or roofing sealant.

MOTHER NATURE (PREPARING FOR FOUL WEATHER)

As a builder of a tiny structure, your primary goal is protecting the contents within—from rain, snow, and wind (or perhaps hail, sleet, or tumbleweeds, depending on your climate). The trickiest part is keeping out water, for which there are some very simple solutions. There are equally simple solutions for dealing with snow and wind. All will help keep your stored items safe and dry no matter the weather. Also, be sure to read the discussion about outdoor finishes in Painting & Staining on page 39.

READY FOR RAIN

It's called rain*fall* for a reason: rain goes down, moving from one surface to the next on its way to the ground. If it lands on a horizontal (or nearly horizontal) surface, it'll just go sideways until it starts going down again. Rain (and melting snow) needs guidance. If you don't direct it where you want it to go, it'll find its way inside your structure and onto its contents.

An inexperienced builder may think that a door keeps out rain. But the door has a top edge, which serves as a landing pad for water, and from there it's just a short trip to the crack between the door and the wall of the structure, and then into the door opening. You have to direct the rain away from the top edge of the door so it doesn't have a chance of landing there. You can do this with an overhanging roof or with a simple piece of molding called a drip cap.

A drip cap has a sloped top face that works like a little awning to shed water away from the door. It also usually has a narrow groove cut into its bottom face. This "drip edge" demonstrates an important lesson about water. Water travels via gravity, but it's also subject to liquid adhesion, which makes liquid cling to surfaces even while it's in motion. If you have wet hands and you lift them up while you search around for a towel, only some of the water falls onto the floor; a lot of it runs down your arms and gets your sleeves all wet, thanks to liquid adhesion.

The same thing happens on a building. Water can run down to the edge of a sloped or vertical surface and, instead of dropping off, take a turn and travel horizontally along the

An extended roof edge or eave keeps water away from the top edge of a door. Note that the roof should slope down over the door like an awning.

ABOVE LEFT: Drip-cap molding installed above a door is a handy alternative to an overhanging roof. **ABOVE RIGHT:** A roof overhang, a drip cap, and a door that overlaps the door opening will keep out blowing snow. This library has all three!

bottom of the same material. The drip edge makes the water fall off so it can't travel to the next vertical surface, such as the wall above a door opening.

Understanding these basics of water behavior helps you when building any kind of structure for weather resistance. And remember this: If water *can* get in, it *will* get in. In addition to directing water away from your door, watch out for entrance points, like roof joints, and for flat areas that can collect water. Caulk any joints or seams that you can't cover up, and avoid flat areas whenever possible.

SIZING FOR SNOW

If you live in snow country, you've surely had the experience of moving an object under a cover, like a porch or carport roof, thinking the snow won't fall there. But you're forgetting that snow doesn't just fall—it also flies. You're reminded of this when all the stuff you put under shelter gets dusted at best and buried under a drift at worst.

Keeping blowing snow out of your shelter is easy. You just need a healthy overlap around all edges of the door and a drip cap or downsloping roof overhang over the door (the same thing that keeps out rain). The easiest door installation is an *overlay*, in which the door overlaps the entire opening. A door that's 1½ inches wider and taller than the opening creates a ¾-inch overlap all around. That's plenty for keeping out snow.

If you're more ambitious and would like to build an *inset* door, or flush door, that sits inside the opening, you can install trim on the interior side of the door wall (so you don't see it when the door is closed), or you can add some flat trim around the outside of the door. The trim overlaps the opening to cover the gaps around the door.

Next is snow depth. Your structure will see a lot less action if it's buried under snow, so try to mount it higher than the average big snowfall in your area.

There's no need to plan for the occasional blizzard, lest your structure be so high that it's hard to reach. A height of 3 feet or so (from the ground to the bottom of the structure) works well in most snowy climates.

WIND

Wind can blow open the door, causing damage itself or letting in the rain or snow. A strong magnetic catch or a simple latch, such as a hook and eye or barrel bolt, secures the door without barring entrance to visitors. Some old salvaged hardware or a homemade wood turn button might work just as well and can add a personal touch.

HELPFUL TOOLS & TECHNIQUES

While there is certainly truth to the old saw *There's a proper tool for every job*, simple woodworking projects give you some flexibility. For example, the best tool for a long, straight cut in plywood is a tablesaw, but you can get by just fine with a circular saw, a jigsaw, or even a handsaw, if you know some tricks for keeping the saw straight. With that example in mind, the following are some common tasks you'll likely run into with your project, along with your options for tools and how to make the most of them.

A latch secures your door against wind and can be a fun custom detail.

MAKING STRAIGHT CUTS

Saws are like children: without guidance, they tend to wander. It takes a very practiced hand to make a long, straight cut with a circular saw or jigsaw.

The longest cuts you'll make will most likely be in plywood. A circular saw is the standard tool for this job, but a jigsaw works just as well. Keeping the saw straight not only yields a straight edge; it also helps minimize splintering along the edges of the cut, a common problem with plywood. When appearance counts, cut from the back side of the plywood so that most of the splintering is on the back face rather than the front.

To make straight cuts in plywood, first mark the cutting line. Then, measure the distance between the saw's blade and the outside edge of the saw's base. Using this dimension, clamp a straightedge—such as a straight board or a 2- or 4-foot level—over the workpiece so it is the same distance from the cutting line. Make the cut, keeping the saw base flush against the straightedge throughout the cut.

If you're using a jigsaw, use a fine-tooth wood blade and set the saw for little or no orbital action to minimize splintering. With a circular saw, a sharp blade splinters less than a dull blade. Also, don't move either saw too fast, which increases splintering.

You can also use a straightedge guide with a handsaw. In this case, use a board for the straightedge and position it just to one side of the cutting line. Make the cut with the saw blade running flush against the board.

MAKING CURVES AND INTERIOR CUTOUTS

ABOVE: Position the straightedge guide so the saw cuts along the cutting line when the saw base is up against the guide. BELOW: Starter holes give your saw's blade a place to begin and make it easy to turn a 90° or sharper corner.

Curves and interior cuts (cuts that start inside a piece rather than at an edge) are best made with a jigsaw. In fact, that's one of the primary tasks jigsaws are made for. Two handsaws that make curves and cutouts are the keyhole saw (also called a compass saw) and a coping saw. Do not confuse a keyhole saw with a similarly shaped tool called a drywall saw. The latter has coarse teeth that make rough, ugly cuts in wood. Coping saws can make very tight curves but are limited in reach.

Make a starter hole for inserting the saw blade to initiate an interior cut. Choose a drill bit slightly larger than the width of the saw blade. Drill a starter hole at each corner of the cutout area, staying on the inside of the cutting lines. Insert the saw blade into the hole and begin cutting.

For a circle or any shape with gentle curves, you may need only one starting hole. For cutouts with squared corners, it's best to drill a starter hole at each corner so the saw blade can turn the corner easily.

TIP: Prevent splintering on the bottom face of the wood (a condition called tearout) by clamping the workpiece on top of a piece of scrap wood (called a sacrificial board because you will drill into it) before drilling the starter holes.

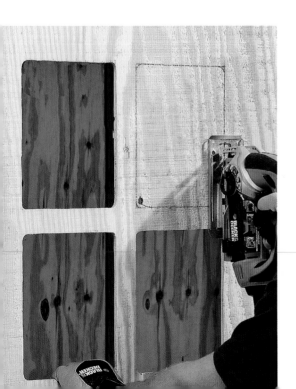

CUTTING TRIM

Trim molding and other small wood parts are best cut with a miter saw of some kind. A miter saw makes straight, clean, repeatable cuts at a variety of angles, and it guides the saw blade throughout the cut. There are two types of miter saws: power and manual. Power miter saws are semiportable machines that make flawless cuts and are actually quite easy to use. If you can borrow one, do it.

Manual miter saws, or miter boxes, consist of a rectangular-bladed handsaw (called a backsaw) and a plastic or metal "box" with a base and two vertical sides. The sides have slots for holding the saw blade at a few different angles, usually 90, 45, and sometimes 22½ degrees. The most basic type of miter box and saw are sold as a kit for as little as $10. These work just fine for occasional use, but they limit you to two or three angles, so you can't make custom cuts.

If you don't have a miter saw or miter box, you can use a square to mark a complete cutting line at the desired angle and then make the cut with a handsaw or backsaw (a hacksaw works too). For small trim, it helps to clamp the workpiece on top of a sacrificial board. This holds the work securely and prevents it from breaking off as you near the end of the cut.

SCREWING AND NAILING IN WOOD

One of the most common mistakes made by beginner builders is failing to drill pilot holes for screws or nails. A pilot hole has a slightly smaller diameter than the screw or nail and makes it much easier to drive the fastener. And because it removes some wood before the fastener goes in, a pilot hole helps prevent splitting. Pilot holes are helpful with most sizes of fasteners, but they're most important with large screws and when nailing or screwing through thin pieces of wood or near the ends or edges of boards.

Drill nail pilot holes with a standard straight drill bit that's slightly smaller than the shank (or shaft) of the nail. Make the hole depth close to the length of the nail shank. If you need to drive the nail at an angle, drill the pilot hole at that angle and the nail will follow it precisely.

BELOW LEFT: Power miter saws can cut any angle from 0° to 45° or so. They're also handy for cutting board lumber and other materials such as plastic pipe and some metals. BELOW MIDDLE: Inexpensive miter boxes are helpful for cutting a few preset angles. BELOW RIGHT: Cut custom angles with a handsaw or backsaw (if you don't have a power miter saw).

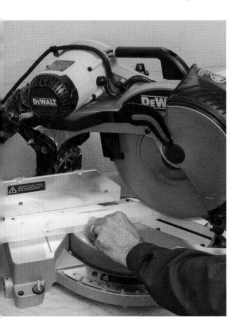
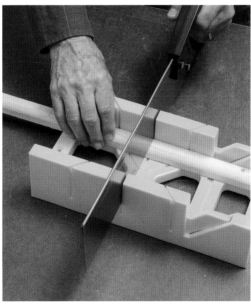

For a finished look, set the heads of finish nails below the wood surface using a punchlike tool called a nail set. Use a nail set with a point that's slightly smaller than the nail head. Place the nail set point onto the nail head and give it two or three hard taps with a hammer until the head is about 1/16 inch below the surface. Fill the hole above the nail head with wood putty and let it dry. Then sand the area smooth to prepare for paint or stain.

Screw pilot holes are drilled with a bit about the same size as the screw's shank, the smooth core around which the threads spiral; this leaves plenty of wood for the threads to bite into. You can use a straight bit for these pilot holes, but a better tool is a combination pilot-countersink bit. This drills a straight pilot hole with a little cup-shaped recess, called a countersink, at the surface. The screw head fits into the countersink for a clean, flush installation. Without a countersink, it can be difficult to get the screw head flush with the wood (especially with hardwood or in an area with knots), and often the wood puckers or splinters a bit.

Pilot-countersink bits are commonly sold in sets containing a few different sizes. There are also versions with adjustable countersinks, and these can be fitted onto standard straight drill bits and tightened with a setscrew. As with finish nails, you can drive screw heads below the surface, then cover the heads with wood putty before painting.

When screwing or nailing through one piece and into the edge of another piece, position the fasteners (and pilot holes) so they are centered along the thickness of the second piece. For example, if you're joining the front wall to the sidewall of a box made with 3/4-inch-thick plywood, you should drive the fasteners 3/8 inch from the edge of the front wall. This means the fasteners will go into the middle of the 3/4-inch edge of the sidewall.

MAKING DOORS WITH (OR WITHOUT) RABBETS

While it may indeed be fun to build things with rodents, a *rabbet* is something completely different. It's a classic woodworkers' term for a square or L-shaped notch cut along the edge of a piece of wood. In the case of doors, a rabbet runs along the inside of the doorframe, creating a recess for laying in the glazing. The glazing is then secured in place with wood strips (called stops) that fit into the remaining space of the rabbet. (Glazing can also be secured in rabbets with caulk.)

Several projects in this book have doorframes with rabbets. They're a little bit tricky to cut, but they make for a nice, professional-looking installation. However, you can simply ignore the rabbets and fasten the door glazing to the back side of the frame using a few screws at the back and a little bit of caulk where the glazing meets the edges of the frame.

There a are few common ways to cut a rabbet. A tablesaw is the standard woodworkers' choice because it can make a lot of cuts quickly and consistently without dulling the blade much. If you don't own a tablesaw, you can also cut rabbets with a router or even a circular saw.

Cutting rabbets with a router is made very easy with a rabbeting bit. A little wheel called a pilot bearing at the bottom of the bit rides along the edge of the wood while the bit's cutting blades make the cut. The width (side to side) of the cut is set by the bearing, while the depth (top to bottom) is adjustable by changing the bit height. You can make several passes as needed to cut deep rabbets. For example, a ½-inch rabbeting bit cuts a ½-inch-wide rabbet at whatever depth you need.

Cutting rabbets with a circular saw is a little trickier than with a router, but it'll do if that's all you have. Start by marking full-length lines for the width and depth of the rabbet. Set the saw blade to cut the desired depth. For the projects in this book, most of the rabbets are ½ inch wide and ½ inch deep. Place the workpiece onto your bench next to an extra piece of matching stock to provide a level surface for the base of the saw; this way, you won't have to balance the saw on a narrow edge. Clamp the pieces securely and make the cut. Flip the workpiece 90 degrees and cut the other half of the rabbet using the same technique.

BELOW: A pilot-countersink bit makes a pilot hole and countersink in a quick operation. **BOTTOM:** Drive screws and nails into the center of plywood edges or other thin or narrow materials.

CUTTING AND DRILLING PLASTIC GLAZING

Acrylic and polycarbonate sheets can be cut and drilled much like wood, but a few tips help prevent chipping, cracking, or melting of these plastic materials. To prevent scratches on your new glazing, don't remove the protective plastic film from either side of the sheeting until all your work is done; ideally, you should leave it on until after the glazing is installed. If there's no plastic film, cover the vulnerable areas with blue painter's tape, which will be easy to remove later.

The most basic way to cut plastic sheeting is by scoring it with a utility knife, using a straightedge to ensure a straight score line. Score the plastic three or more times, then hold or clamp the sheet so the scored line is directly above the edge of a workbench or table. Snap the overhanging portion down sharply to break the sheet at the scored line.

The best way to cut plastic sheeting is with a jigsaw and a blade designed for plastic or with a fine-tooth blade for metal. Run the saw at a slow speed

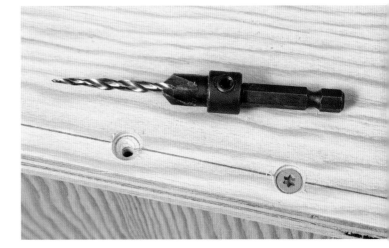

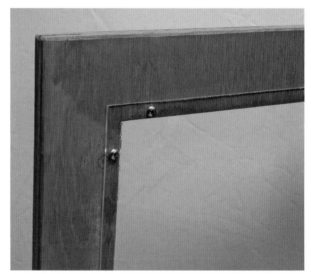

TOP AND INSET: The pilot bearing on a rabbeting bit rides along the edge of the wood to control the width of the cut. **ABOVE LEFT:** Rabbets create a recess in an assembled frame for accepting the glazing and stops. **ABOVE RIGHT:** The rabbet alternative: Screw the glazing to the back of the assembled doorframe and run a thin bead of clear caulk along the front edges of the frame.

(with no orbital action) and move it slowly and steadily through the cut. If you move the saw too quickly, the plastic can melt and fuse back together behind the blade. Let the saw get up to speed before starting the cut, and be extra careful when finishing the cut, as this is a weak spot that can easily chip.

Another option is a circular saw with a fine-tooth blade. As with a jigsaw, move the saw slowly to prevent overheating and chipping. It's a good idea to use a straightedge guide (see Making Straight Cuts on page 31) to keep the saw straight. Also, set the blade depth so it cuts just below the depth of the plastic; setting the blade too low creates unnecessary friction and heat. Wear safety glasses and hearing protection!

Drill holes in plastic glazing using a power drill and standard drill bits or a step drill bit, a graduated cone-shaped bit that drills holes of increasingly larger sizes, one size at a time. Use a moderately slow drill speed and don't force the bit through the material. Support the glazing with a sacrificial board under the area to be drilled, and clamp the glazing to the board so it won't move. With a sharp bit, holes are clean and almost effortless, but carelessness or rushing the work will crack the material.

For large holes over about ⅛ inch in diameter, start with a small hole, then drill progressively larger holes to gradually work up to the desired hole size. This helps prevent cracking. Alternatively, you can use a step bit. This does the same thing as using increasingly larger bits but requires only one bit. A step bit usually doesn't require a sacrificial board, but the plastic should be well supported near the hole site.

Holes drilled in glazing for screws should be about 1⅓ times the size of the screw shank to allow room for the plastic to expand and contract. For example, for a ³⁄₁₆-inch-diameter screw, drill a ¼-inch-diameter pilot hole. Also, use screws with a flat surface under the head; don't use bugle-head screws (such as drywall screws) or flathead screws with a conical shape under the head.

LEFT: Step bits are commonly used to drill holes in thin metals. They're pricey but less likely to crack plastic glazing than standard drill bits. **BELOW:** Only a jigsaw can cut curves in plastic sheeting. Use a fine-tooth blade (for plastic or metal), not a wood blade, which can chip or crack the plastic. **BOTTOM:** Support the glazing with a flat sacrificial board and drill straight down through the plastic and into the board to complete each hole.

WORKING WITH SHEET METAL

Working with sheet metal is surprisingly similar to working with paper. Both materials are cut with scissorlike tools and are bent and folded to make neat corners. Creasing and folding takes a little more effort with metal, but the basic geometric principles are the same. One key difference is sharpness: while paper can deliver the universally dreaded paper cut, sheet metal cuts can easily require stitches. Wear heavy leather gloves whenever working with sheet metal. If there will be exposed edges in the finished product, file them smooth, or fold the edge under to create a hem and hammer it flat so the cut edge is underneath the surface.

HOW TO CUT SHEET METAL

Mark the cutting line with a square or straightedge and a fine marker or a pencil. Make the cut with aviation snips. If the cut is long, carefully lift up the upper portion of the material to allow the snips to stay straight (photo 1). This can be tricky at times. Lift the piece as high as you can without creasing the metal. At some point, it might be easier to stop cutting in one direction and complete the cut from the opposite direction.

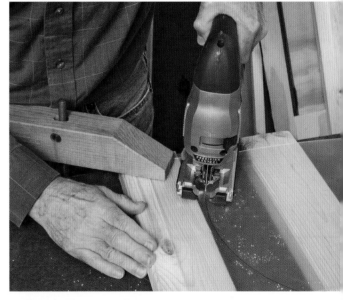

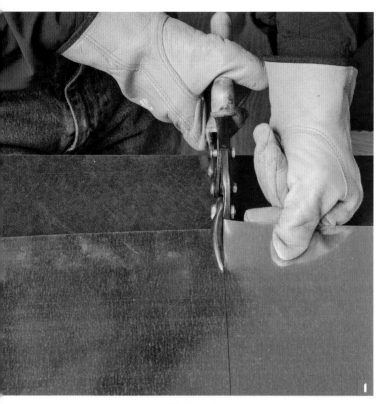

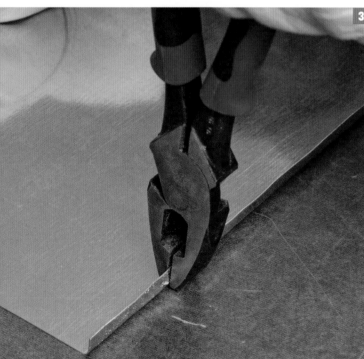

HOW TO MAKE A SEAM IN SHEET METAL

1. Lift and gently bend the loose piece of metal to make room for the snip's blades. 2. Bend the sheet metal over a crisp edge of your work surface.
3. Bend narrow edges further with flat-nose pliers or linesman's pliers. 4. Flatten seams with a standard (smooth-faced) hammer.

HOW TO BEND SHEET METAL

Place the sheet so it overhangs the edge of your worksurface. The edge of the surface is where the bend will be. **Note:** The edge of the worksurface should be straight and sharp, like the edge of a cut board, not rounded over like the edge of a 2 × 4. If you don't have a workbench with a good edge, clamp a piece of plywood to a table so it overhangs the edge of the table.

Bend the metal straight down to follow the edge of the worksurface (photo 2). It's best to bend by hand whenever possible, but if the overhang is narrow, you may need to hammer the overhang to make the bend. When hammering, keep the face of the hammerhead flat to the metal (so you don't make dents), and avoid hammering directly over the workbench edge (which will dent your crease).

If you're making a 90-degree bend and it's not quite there, lift the metal from the worksurface and bend the edge a bit further by hand or with flat-nose pliers (photo 3). You can also use linesman's pliers (preferably) or regular slip-joint pliers (if they have relatively flat, wide jaws).

If you're making a hem (folded-over edge), bend the edge as far as possible with flat-nose pliers, then place the edge flat on your worksurface and hammer it flat (photo 4). Keep the face of the hammerhead flat to prevent dents. Use short hammer strokes and work the edge until the hem lies flat and the crease is crisp and straight.

PAINTING & STAINING

Unless you're building a really rustic structure that's supposed to weather like an old barn, you'll want to protect all exposed wood materials with an exterior finish. A finish protects wood from moisture and ultraviolet (UV) light. Moisture causes wood to swell and split and promotes decay. UV light breaks down lignin, the binder that holds wood fibers together, leaving the wood gray, rough, and splintery.

Remember that all outdoor finishes must be touched up or recoated periodically to maintain the protective layer and to keep the finish from getting old and brittle. See Painting & Staining on pages 40–41 for more information on maintaining finishes. Choose a finish based on the type of wood you're protecting and the overall look you're going for:

Paint: Paint is best for solid colors that cover the underlying wood completely. Use high-quality exterior house paint. The best formulas tend to be 100 percent acrylic. If a paint says "acrylic-latex," it's probably not 100 percent acrylic. *Latex* is a nebulous industry term that indicates a water-based paint, as opposed to oil- or alkyd-based. Latex paint may contain acrylic, vinyl, or other synthetic polymers. What it doesn't contain is natural latex. Paint with 100 percent acrylic binders dries harder and generally lasts longer than vinyl and blended formulas.

Paint or stain as directed by the manufacturer. A small sash brush is great for the trim and tight spots on little structures.

PAINTING & STAINING FAQs

How much do I need to sand wood before painting or staining?

Sanding wood before finishing removes scratches, saw marks, splinters, sharp edges, and unsightly rough areas. If you don't sand, these blemishes will show in the finished project. Always start with the lowest grit of sandpaper and work up to finer grits. (The higher the grit number the finer the paper—and the smoother the wood gets.)

For rough surfaces and deep scratches, start with 60- or 80-grit paper, but be careful not to remove too much wood, especially when sanding the thin face layers of plywood. Move up to 100- or 120-grit for a medium sand, then up to 150- or 180-grit for a final sanding. In most cases, there's no need to sand with anything finer than 180-grit sandpaper. In fact, painting is best after sanding with 150-grit, and staining can be splotchy if you sand with finer than 220-grit.

Should I prepaint or prestain the wood parts or wait until the structure is assembled?

There are pros and cons to both approaches. Finishing the parts before assembly makes it easier to reach all the faces and edges of parts, and it eliminates working in tight corners. It also allows you to paint different colors on adjacent parts without having to tape anything off.

On the downside, wood glue is designed to bond to bare wood, not to paint or stain. Glued joints are much stronger if they're made when the wood is unfinished. Paint also adds some thickness to parts, so prepainting sometimes can result in parts not fitting as they should. Finally, painted projects look best (and last longer) if the joints are caulked, and usually you have to paint after you caulk, for appearance.

As a compromise, you can prefinish some or all parts but keep the finish away from all surfaces to be glued. You can also save the final coat until after the parts are assembled and the joints are caulked (if painting).

Do painted projects need a primer?

The textbook answer is yes. Primer is sticky, cheap paint that bonds well with bare wood and provides a flat, white base for covering with top coats of paint in any color. Primer helps hide knots and other blemishes and prevents your good paint from soaking in, so you don't have to use as much of the expensive stuff. Those benefits aside, you can skip primer if you want, but you might need an extra coat of paint for good coverage.

Should I finish the interior of my structure?

It's a very good idea but not necessarily required. Finishing the interior makes the wood more moisture- and stain-resistant and much easier to clean. It also can help prevent warping of the wood due to moisture affecting one side of the material more than the other. A painted interior will get marked and scuffed over the years, but it can be touched up periodically. Be sure to let the paint cure fully (not just dry) before adding items. Fresh paint stays sticky for several days and can stick to objects resting on it.

What kind of clear coat finish do I need?

If you go with a urethane or similar film-forming clear coat, choose a good-quality acrylic formula with UV inhibitors. For a penetrating sealer, look for a product with a high solids content (compare labels). You might also consider a hybrid formula that soaks into the wood with the first coat and creates a protective film with the second coat.

Does it make sense to add a sealer over paint or stain?

Some sources recommend applying a clear coat over paint or stain, but there's little benefit to this. Exterior paint and stain are designed to be a top coat, protective finish themselves; they don't need another protective finish on top. If you do add a clear coat over paint or stain, you'll have to maintain the clear coat just as much as you would the paint or stain. One exception is using a clear coat to protect painted artwork (see Protecting Painted Artwork on page 42).

Can oily rags really spontaneously combust?

Just sneaking in a safety warning here: oily rags can indeed start their own fires without the addition of sunlight, heat, matches, or anything other than a small amount of oxygen. Oils in many stains and other finish materials cure through a chemical reaction called oxidation that creates heat. If you trap the heat by balling or piling up the rags, the rags can catch fire. Better to let oily rags dry by laying them out in a single layer outdoors or submerging them in water in a metal container with a tight-fitting lid.

Paint is the classic choice for color. Look for exterior paint in small sample containers (7 ounces or so) available at hardware stores and home centers.

Stain: Most exterior stains are oil-based formulas and are commonly applied to wood decks, fences, and house siding. Stains come in three basic levels of pigment, or opaqueness: transparent, semitransparent (also called semiopaque), and solid body (also called solid color). Transparent stain adds some color but is very thin and soaks into the wood, allowing the woodgrain to show. At the other end of the spectrum, solid body stain completely obscures the wood's natural coloring, but it goes on thinner and retains a bit more of the wood's texture than paint. Semiopaque stain is somewhere in between, both in pigment and thickness. The more pigment a stain has, the better it protects the wood from UV light.

Clear coat: Use a clear coat when you want the wood to look as natural as possible, without the coloring of a stain or paint. Clear coats come in two basic types: film-forming (urethanes and varnishes) and penetrating (oil-based sealers). The primary challenge for clear coats is UV protection. Paints and stains use pigment to block sunlight and prevent it from reaching the wood. Clear coats, which have little or no pigment, must use UV inhibitors that work like sunblock lotion. But as with sunblock, they're effective for a limited time; you must reapply the coating every one or two years to maintain the finish. Clear coats typically are used over bare wood, but they're also effective for protecting painted artwork without obscuring it (see below).

PROTECTING PAINTED ARTWORK

If you add painted artwork or other custom details to your structure—things that you don't want to redo every few years—you should protect the painted finish with a clear coat of some kind. You still need to refresh the clear coat periodically, but with proper maintenance you'll keep your original masterpiece intact.

A lasting finish starts with the first coat. For the artwork, use a good-quality outdoor acrylic craft paint. Like standard exterior paint, outdoor craft paint is designed to last without a separate top coat, but by adding a clear coat you create a "wear layer" that can be sanded or screened and recoated as needed without affecting the artwork beneath. The important thing is to use a clear coat that's nonyellowing and is compatible with the craft paint. Ask the paint manufacturer to recommend specific products that will work with your paint.

Project Plans

It's time to build! Each of the twelve projects in this chapter includes a construction drawing, tools and materials list, cutting list, and step-by-step instructions and photos to walk you through the project from start to finish. The projects are arranged in no particular order, and some are a bit more complicated than others, but the first one is undoubtedly the easiest. That's because it uses a kit from Little Free Library. You can order the same kit, complete with all of the necessary parts, and use the instructions provided here to assemble it.

The other projects show you how to build each structure from scratch, using standard materials you can find at any lumberyard or home center. And that brings us to an important note on materials. Experienced builders know that materials can vary from brand to brand, from store to store, and even from stack to stack. The sizes of materials, particularly wood, are not universal. Plywood that's called "⅝-inch" often isn't exactly ⅝ inch thick. And 2 × 4s never measure 2 inches by 4 inches; they typically measure about 1½ inches by 3½ inches (it's a long story).

With this in mind, remember to take some time to pore over your project drawing and cutting list, and compare the dimensions in the cutting list with the actual dimensions of your own materials. If you find some variation, don't sweat it. You can refer to the drawing and the project steps to learn where each part goes, and you can cut specific parts to fit rather than follow the given dimensions. For example, if the plans call for a piece of trim that covers the edge of a plywood box, and your plywood is slightly thicker than the specified material (so that cutting the trim to the given dimension would leave it a little short), just measure your box and cut the trim to the measured size.

As for the project designs, you can follow the plans to a tee or use them for inspiration and consider them a jumping-off point for your own ideas. Each project includes a photo of the finished structure. The colors, the contents, and even the themes presented are merely suggestions. Feel free to modify, embellish, decorate, resize, or reshape. Making all those executive (or artistic) decisions is the beauty of building your own structure.

LittleFreeLibrary.org®
Take a Book · Return a Book
A Nonprofit Organization

Learn how to register your Little Free Library on page 156.

One-Story Shed Kit

The One-Story Shed is sold by Little Free Library as both a kit and a completely assembled structure. The kit is particularly popular with groups that host volunteer building events— or "build days"—during which participants get together to assemble a number of kits for donation. The kit comes complete with all the screws and nails for assembly, and all the wood parts are precut and predrilled. Even the door is installed and already features a Little Free Library charter sign. This makes for a fun and quick assembly, so you can turn your attention to the even more fun job of painting (or staining) and decorating. (Yes, the kit parts are unfinished.)

The assembled One-Story Shed measures 21 inches wide × 19 inches deep × 23 inches tall and has a roomy interior space that can accommodate books of almost any size. The door has a large Plexiglas panel within a solid-wood frame. One of the best features of this design is the traditional drip cap molding above the door. This gives the facade its distinctive architectural look and does a good job of protecting the top of the door from rain and snow.

Most of the One-Story Shed's materials are standard for this type of structure: ⅝-inch plywood for the walls, floor, and roof, and solid pine lumber for the trim, cleats, and doorframe. The only part that's not so standard is the roofing—a single sheet of asphalt roofing trimmed on all sides with painted aluminum angle. Don't be surprised if this outlasts the roof on your home!

INSTRUCTIONS

Check the Kit Contents

Unwrap the kit package and lay out all the parts. Check all the items against the parts list to ensure nothing is missing. If any parts are missing or damaged, contact the sender as soon as possible.

Dry-Assemble the Shed

A dry run is helpful for visualizing the finished product and should make the actual assembly—with glue—go more smoothly. You may want to use bar clamps or a helper to hold the pieces together for the dry run and for the final assembly.

Start by standing up the front-door panel, then the two side panels. Position the side panels against the inside face of the front panel, on the inside of the front-panel corner trim. The cleats (lumber strips) at the top edges of the side

1. The roof cleat rests against the front edge of the rear panel. 2. If you are prefinishing your project, trace lightly with a pencil to mark where the mating pieces overlap. 3. Drive 2″ screws through the predrilled holes in the front panel and into the side panels.

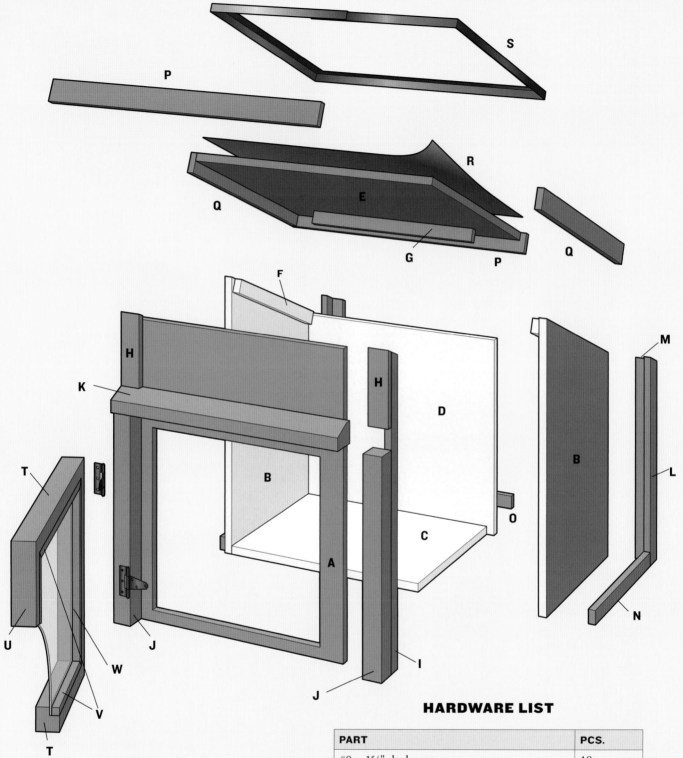

HARDWARE LIST

PART	PCS.
#8 × 1⅝" deck screws	18
#8 × 2½" deck screws	6
1" trim nails	15
Doorknob (with bolt)	1
Hinges	2

TOOLS & MATERIALS

Tools & Materials to Assemble Kit:
(2) bar clamps (optional; at least 18" capacity)
Rosin paper or newspaper (optional)
Hammer
Drill-driver and #2 Phillips screwdriver bit
Waterproof wood glue

Eye and ear protection
Work gloves
Little Free Library charter sign

Materials Used in Kit:
4 × 4' sheet of ⁹⁄₃₂" plywood
¾ × 1 × 42" pine
(2) ½ × 1½ × 96" pine
1⅜ × 1½ × 30" pine

1½ × 1⅞ × 18¼" pine drip cap
½ × 1 × 96" pine
19¼ × 20⅞" asphalt roofing
¾ × ¾ × 85" light-gauge metal angle
1½ × 1¹¹⁄₁₆ × 60" pine
½ × ½ × 48" pine
⅛ × 11⅞ × 12⅞" acrylic glazing
½ × ¾ × 2½" pine

PARTS LIST

KEY	PART	DIMENSIONS	PCS.	MATERIAL
A	Front door panel	⁹⁄₃₂ × 17¼ × 20¾"	1	Plywood
B	Side panel	⁹⁄₃₂ × 13 × 20¾"	2	Plywood
C	Base	⁹⁄₃₂ × 13 × 16"	1	Plywood
D	Back	⁹⁄₃₂ × 17⅛ × 15"	1	Plywood
E	Roof deck	⁹⁄₃₂ × 18½ × 20"	1	Plywood
F	Roof cleat—side panel	¾ × 1 × 13¼"	2	Pine
G	Roof cleat—roof deck	¾ × 1 × 14³⁄₁₆"	1	Pine
H	Front-panel trim—front	½ × 1½ × 5⅛"	2	Pine
I	Front-panel trim—side	½ × 1 × 21"	2	Pine
J	Front panel—doorpost	1⅜ × 1½ × 14⁷⁄₁₆"	2	Pine
K	Front panel—drip cap	1½ × 1⅞ × 18¼"	1	Pine
L	Rear-corner trim—side	½ × 1½ × 15½"	2	Pine
M	Rear-corner trim—rear	½ × 1 × 15⅛"	2	Pine
N	Side trim	½ × 1 × 12⅛"	2	Pine
O	Lower rear-facing trim	½ × 1 × 15¹⁄₁₆"	1	Pine
P	Roof trim—front/rear	½ × 1½ × 21"	2	Pine
Q	Roof trim—side	½ × 1½ × 18½"	2	Pine
R	Roofing	19¼ × 20⅞"	1	Asphalt roofing
S	Roof metal edge	¾ × ¾ × 85"	1	Metal angle
T	Doorframe—top/bottom	1½ × 1¹¹⁄₁₆ × 15⅛"	2	Pine
U	Doorframe—side	1½ × 1¹¹⁄₁₆ × 14⅛"	2	Pine
V	Door glazing stop—top/bottom	½ × ½ × 12⅞"	2	Pine
W	Door glazing stop—side	½ × ½ × 11⅞"	2	Pine
X	Door glazing	⅛ × 11⅞ × 12⅞"	1	Acrylic glazing
Y	Door turn button	½ × ¾ × 2½"	1	Pine

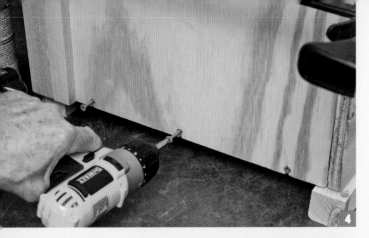

panels should be on the inside of the assembly, and the points at the top of the side panels should be flush with the top edge of the front panel.

Slide the base between the side panels and up against the front-door panel. Position the back panel over the rear edges of the side panels and base; the long horizontal side of the back panel that has predrilled screw holes should face the base. If desired, you can clamp both sides from front to back to hold the box together.

Fit the roof onto the box assembly. The underside of the roof has a wood cleat; this goes in front of the back panel (photo 1). Center the roof from side to side to complete the dry assembly.

Option: Prefinish the Shed

You have the option of painting or staining your shed before or after it's assembled. To make prefinishing easier, remove the door and its hinges, and apply painter's tape to cover both sides of the door glazing (Plexiglas). While you have the shed dry-assembled, mark light pencil lines where all of the box pieces overlap (photo 2). This will mark off the surfaces that will be glued; leave these unfinished (as well as the front, back, and top edges of the side panels) to ensure strong glue joints with the final assembly (glue sticks much better to bare wood than to painted or stained wood).

Assemble the Front, Sides, and Base

Now it's time for the final assembly. It's important to work on a flat surface so the pieces align properly. If desired, cover the surface with rosin paper or newspaper to protect it from glue.

Apply wood glue to the front (long) edges of the side panels and to the front and both side edges of the base. Position the side panels against the glued side edges of the base so all three pieces are flush at the front. Position the front-door panel against the side panels and base, as in the dry assembly. Have a helper hold the pieces together or clamp them with bar clamps.

Fasten the front panel to each side panel with three 2½-inch screws driven through the front panel and into the edge of the side panel using a drill-driver and #2 Phillips screwdriver bit (photo 3). Fasten the side panels to the base with three 1⅝-inch screws on each side, driving through the sides and into the base (photo 4).

ROOF

4. Fasten the sides to the base with three 1⅝" screws on each side.
5. Screw through the back panel and into the side panels and base with 1⅝" screws. 6. Nail the corner trim into the edge of the back panel with 1" trim nails. 7. Center the box assembly on the roof and fasten the roof with screws on the inside of the shed.

Install the Back Panel

Apply glue to the rear edges of the side panels and the base. Fit the back panel into place so its long horizontal edge with the predrilled screw holes faces the base. Make sure the side edges of the back are flush with the outside edges of the side panels. The bottom edge of the back should be flush with the bottom face of the base.

Fasten the back panel to the side panels and base with 1⅝-inch screws driven through the predrilled holes in the back panel (photo 5).

Add the Rear Corner Trim

Apply glue to the inside faces of one of the rear corner trim assemblies. Position the trim over the corner of the back and side panels so the top edge of the trim is flush with the top edge of the side panel (the trim and side panels have matching angles).

Fasten the trim to the rear panel with three 1-inch trim nails (photo 6). Drive one nail about 1½ inches from both ends, and drive the third nail centered in between. This ensures you won't hit any of the screws securing the back panel to the side panel. Repeat the same process to install the corner trim piece on the other rear corner of the shed.

Install the Roof

Place the roof top-side down on your worksurface. Apply glue to the top edges of the side panels, including the side panel cleats. Flip the box assembly upside down and place it onto the roof so the cleat on the roof rests against the inside face of the back panel (photo 7). Measure outward from both sides of the side panels to make sure the roof overhangs both sides equally.

Open the door to the shed, reach inside with the drill, and drive 1⅝-inch screws through the side panel cleats and into the plywood of the roof. Drive three screws on each cleat using the predrilled holes. Flip the shed right-side up.

Add the Remaining Trim

Apply glue to one face of one of the side-trim pieces. Position the trim piece between the rear-corner trim and the corner trim on the front panel. The side trim should be flush with the bottom ends of the corner trim. Fasten the side trim to the side panel with three trim nails, spacing the nails evenly.

Repeat the same process to install the other side trim piece. Install the lower rear-facing trim piece in the same fashion, positioning it between the two rear-corner trim assemblies (photo 8).

Finish the Job

You're done with the main assembly! All that's left is sanding and finishing the project and installing the doorknob and Little Free Library medallion. Let the glue dry for 24 hours after the assembly, then finish the project as desired (see Painting & Staining on pages 39–42 for finishing tips). It helps to remove the door and hinges and tape off the door glazing for the finishing process.

Reinstall the door, and attach the doorknob with the provided bolt (photo 9). Install the Little Free Library medallion, if desired, using the provided screws. Install the One-Story Shed (see Installing Your Structure on pages 137–145), and you're ready to open your Little Free Library to the public!

8. The side and lower rear-facing trim pieces fit snugly between the corner trim assemblies. 9. Insert the bolt for the knob through the predrilled hole in the doorframe.

Learn how to register your Little Free Library on page 156.

Mini Shed

True to its name, the Mini Shed is the smallest of the Little Free Library designs, measuring in at 15½ inches wide × 14 inches deep × 16 inches tall. Its simple box construction makes very good use of this space, yielding a surprisingly large and tall interior for storing most standard-size books or a lot of other items.

The design elements are also pretty simple, making this a good project for beginners. There are a few tricky details—namely, the rabbets in the doorframe (see Making Doors with [or without] Rabbets on page 34) and several trim pieces, which are best cut with a tablesaw. If these cuts are a little too advanced for you, you can follow the suggested workarounds to build the door without rabbets and create the trim by gluing flat pieces together rather than rip-cutting single pieces.

The Mini Shed is ideal for mounting to a post below a larger tiny structure to create a special exchange just for kids. But there's no reason it can't stand on its own post if it's the right size for what you need. Its mini-ness also makes it a good candidate for indoor placement, fitting well on a shelf or a side table or even a desk.

INSTRUCTIONS

Cut the Plywood Parts

Cut the side panels, front panel, back panel, base, and roof deck to size using a circular saw or jigsaw. All of the pieces are rectangular except for the side panels, which have angled top ends. To lay out the angled cut, mark a 9⁹⁄₁₆ × 14¾-inch rectangle, then measure down from the top and mark one long side edge at ⅞ inch. Draw a line from the mark to the opposing top corner, and cut along the line (photo 1).

Note: If you don't want to rabbet the side panels (see next step), cut the side panels to size at 9³⁄₁₆ × 14¹¹⁄₁₆ inches, and cut the front panel to size at 12⁹⁄₁₆ × 14¾ inches. You can also skip the next step. When you assemble the shed box, the front panel will completely cover the front edges of the side panels, rather than fit into the side panel rabbets.

Rabbet the Sides Panels

Cut a ½-inch-wide × ⅜-inch-deep rabbet along the front edge of each side panel using a router and ⅜-inch rabbeting bit (see Making Doors with [or without] Rabbets on page 34 for help with cutting rabbets). The rabbets will receive the ½-inch-thick front panel.

1. Mark trim locations on both side panels. 2. Make the door cutout with a jigsaw, using a starter hole at each corner. 3. Secure the front panel to the box assembly with glue and finish nails.

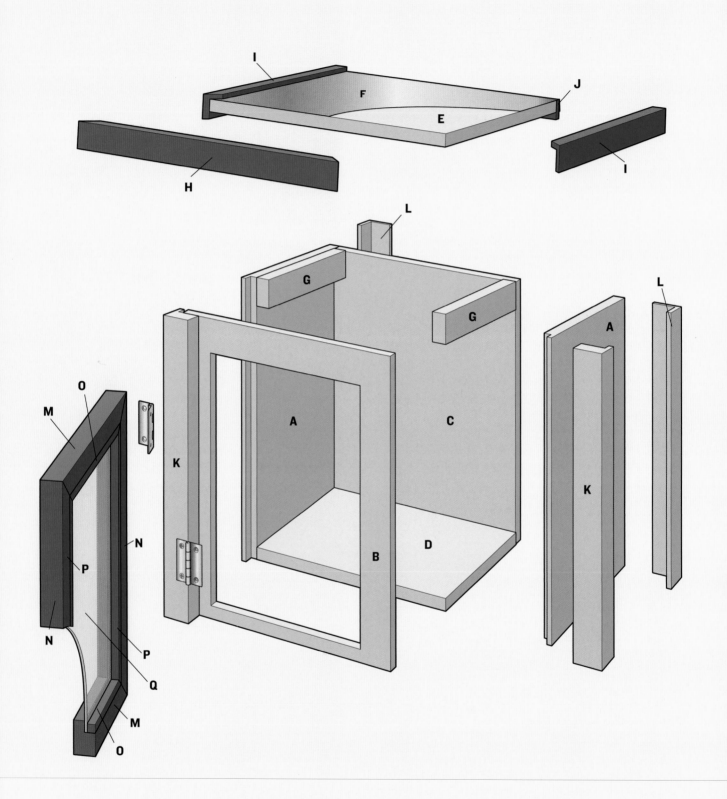

TOOLS & MATERIALS

Circular saw
Jigsaw
Tablesaw (optional)
Router and ⅜" rabbeting bit
  (optional)
Clamps
Straightedge
Drill-driver
Pilot-countersink bit
Screwdriver bits
Drill bits (⅛", ⅜")
Hammer
Nail set
Miter saw or miter box

Aviation snips
Caulking gun
2 × 4' piece of ⅝" plywood
13 × 15" piece of ½" plywood
1 × 2" (nominal) × 6' pine
⅜ × 1 × 15" pine
2 × 2" (nominal) × 8' pine
1 × 1½ × 48" pine
⅜ × ⅜ × 48" pine
14 × 16" piece of 26-gauge
  galvanized steel or aluminum sheet
  metal
⅛ × 8 × 12" acrylic glazing

(6) 1¼" wood screws
(9) 1⅝" trim screws
(6) 1¾" wood screws
(4) 2¼" wood screws
(18) 1¼" finish nails
(24) ¾" finish nails
Waterproof wood glue
(2) 1⅞ × 2½" exterior hinges with
  screws
Construction adhesive
Silicone caulk
Eye and ear protection
Work gloves

CUTTING LIST

KEY	PART	DIMENSIONS	PCS.	MATERIAL
A	Side panel	⅝ × 9⁹⁄₁₆ × 14¾"	2	⅝" plywood
B	Front panel	⁵⁄₁₆ × 12³⁄₆ × 14¾"	1	½" plywood
C	Back panel	⅝ × 11⁷⁄₁₆ × 13⅞"	1	⅝" plywood
D	Base	⅝ × 8⁹⁄₁₆ × 11½"	1	⅝" plywood
E	Roof deck	⅝ × 14⅛ × 13⁹⁄₁₆"	1	⅝" plywood
F	Roofing	14 × 14½"	1	Sheet metal
G	Roof cleat	¾ × 1½ × 8⁹⁄₁₆"	2	Pine
H	Roof trim—top	¾ × 1½ × 14⅞"	1	Pine
I	Roof trim—side	¾ × 1½ × 14⅜"	2	Pine
J	Roof trim—bottom	⅜ × 1 × 14⅛"	1	Pine
K	Front-corner trim	1½ × 1½ × 14¾"	2	Pine
L	Rear-corner trim	¼ × 1½ × 1½"	2	Pine
M	Doorframe—top/bottom	1 × 1½ × 9⅞"	2	Pine
N	Doorframe—side	1 × 1½ × 13⅞"	2	Pine
O	Glazing stop—top/bottom	⅜ × ⅜ × 7¹⁵⁄₁₆"	2	Pine
P	Glazing stop—side	⅜ × ⅜ × 11¹³⁄₁₆"	2	Pine
Q	Door glazing	⅛ × 8 × 12"	1	Acrylic glazing

Cut the Door Opening

The front panel gets a rectangular cutout for the door opening that is $8^{13}/_{16}$ inches wide × $12^{7}/_{16}$ inches tall. Mark this rectangle onto the front panel so it is centered side to side and the bottom of the rectangle is $9/_{16}$ inch from the bottom edge of the panel. Drill a $3/_8$-inch starter hole (or large enough to accommodate the jigsaw blade; see Making Curves and Interior Cutouts on page 32) on the inside of each corner of the rectangle, then make the cutout with a jigsaw (photo 2).

Assemble the Box

Apply wood glue to the side edges of the back panel. Fit the side panels over the glued edges so all pieces are flush at the top and the side panels are flush with the back face of the back panel. Fasten the side panels to the back with three $1^3/_4$-inch screws each.

Glue the sides and rear edges of the plywood base. Fit the base against the side and back panels so all pieces are flush at the bottom. Fasten through the side and back panels and into the base with $1^5/_8$-inch trim screws.

Glue the front edge of the base and inside both rabbeted edges of the side panels. Fit the front panel into the rabbets so all pieces are flush at the top and bottom. Nail through the front panel and into the sides with three $1^1/_4$-inch finish nails on each side. Set the nails using a nail set (photo 3).

4-5. The first rip cut leaves about $1/_4$" of material below the saw blade (left); the second cut is full-depth and creates a $1/_8$"-wide lip (right).

Add the Roof Cleats

Cut the two roof cleats to length from 1×2 lumber, mitering both ends of each piece at 5 degrees using a miter saw or miter box. The miters on each piece should be parallel to each other.

Apply glue to one side face of each roof cleat. Position each cleat against the inside of a side panel, flush with the top edge. Fasten each cleat to the side panel with two $1^1/_4$-inch screws.

Prepare the Front-Corner Trim

The two front-corner trim pieces are cut from 2 × 2 lumber and have a shallow lip along one edge that overlaps the corner of the plywood box. They are also mitered on their top ends at 5 degrees. It's easiest to make the long rip cuts on a 48-inch length of 2 × 2, then cut the trim to final size with a miter saw or miter box. However, if the 2 × 2 lumber isn't very straight, it might be easier to work with shorter pieces.

Cut an 8-foot 2 × 2 in half, then set one of the halves aside; you will use it later for the rear corner trim. To make the first rip cut, set your tablesaw to cut $1^3/_{16}$ inches deep. Make a long rip cut 1 inch from a long side edge of the 2 × 2 (photo 4). (Alternatively, you can mill these rabbets on a router table.)

Reset the saw to cut completely through the 2 × 2, and reset the guide to cut $1/_8$ inch over from the first cut. This will create a $1/_8$-inch-deep lip (photo 5). Finally, cut each trim piece to length, mitering the top end at 5 degrees.

Install the Front-Corner Trim

Apply glue to the back face of each corner trim piece; this is the face with the lip, but do not apply glue to the exposed portion of the lip. Position each trim piece at the front corner of the box assembly so the top (mitered) end of the trim is flush with the top of the box and the lip is up against the side panel. Fasten each trim piece with three 1¼-inch screws driven through the inside of the front panel and into the trim.

Add the Rear-Corner Trim

The rear-corner trim pieces are L-shaped and are cut from the leftover 48-inch piece of 2 × 2. As with the front-corner trim, cutting the Ls here requires two long rip cuts. Make the rip cuts before cutting the trims to final length.

Set your tablesaw to cut a depth of 1⅛ inches and rip the 2 × 2 to make a ⅜-inch-thick leg of the L. Rotate the 2 × 2 and make a second pass to meet the first cut; the piece now has a right-angle shape with two equally wide legs. Finally, rip-cut one of the legs to 1⅛ inches wide, creating an L with one wide leg and one narrow leg (photo 6).

Note: If you prefer not to cut the rear-corner trim from a single piece, you can glue a ¼-inch-thick × 1½-inch-wide piece of pine to a ¼-inch-thick × ¾-inch-wide piece to form an L.

Cut the two trim pieces to final length, mitering the top ends at 5 degrees. Apply glue to the inside faces of the trim. Fit them over the rear corners of the box so the wide leg is against the back panel and all pieces are flush at the top. Fasten the trim with three ¾-inch finish nails through each leg of the L.

Prepare the Roof Trim

The roof trim consists of three pieces of rabbeted pine—for the sides and top of the roof—and one piece of flat molding for the bottom edge of the roof. As with the other rabbeted pieces, you can rabbet a single piece of long stock before cutting the side and top pieces to length.

Cut a ⅜-inch-wide × 1⅛-inch-deep rabbet on a 6-foot length of 1 × 2 pine to create an L-shaped angle. Cut the top roof-trim piece to length, mitering both ends at 45 degrees. Cut each of the two side roof trim pieces to length, with one end square and one end mitered at 45 degrees (photo 7).

Note: If you don't want to rabbet the roof trim, you can create the L-shaped pieces by gluing ¼-inch-thick × ¾-inch-wide pine to the edge of ¼-inch-thick × 1-inch-wide pine. Cut the final trim pieces to length after assembling them.

Cut the bottom roof trim to length from ⅜ × 1-inch pine stock, square-cutting both ends. Apply glue to one face of the trim, and fasten it to the rear (14⅛-inch) edge of the roof deck with three 1¼-inch finish nails. The trim should be flush with the ends and top face of the roof deck.

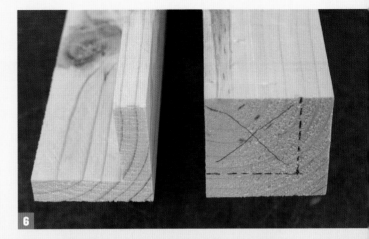

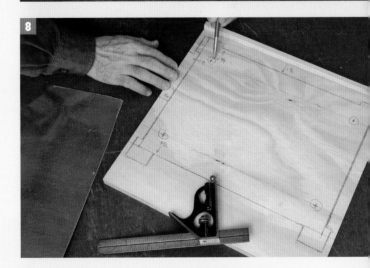

6. The rear-corner trim requires three cuts: two partial-depth cuts to form an angle and a final full-depth cut to make one leg narrower than the other. 7. The side and top roof trim pieces fit together with mitered corners at the top edge of the roof. 8. Drill pilot holes and mark the corners where the box assembly will meet the roof.

9. Caulk along the trim at the sides and front of the roof to prevent water from getting under the trim. 10. Hang the door so it is centered between the front-corner trim pieces.

Prepare the Roof

Cut the sheet-metal roofing to size using aviation snips. Bend the metal along the bottom (14-inch) edge at 90 degrees to create a ½-inch lip (see Working with Sheet Metal on page 37 for help with cutting and bending sheet metal).

Drill four ⅛-inch pilot holes through the roof deck: two front holes 4½ inches from the front edge and 1¾ inches from each side edge; two rear holes 2¾ inches from the rear edge and 1¾ inches from each side edge. Draw corner markers on the bottom side of the roof deck to guide the roof's position on the box. Mark the front corners 3 inches from the front edge and ¾ inches from each side edge, and mark the rear corners 1 inch from the rear edge and ¾ inch from each side edge (photo 8).

Complete the Roof

Apply glue to the top edges of the box assembly and the roof cleats. Place the roof deck on top of the box so the four corner markers align with the corners of the box. The roof will overhang the box about 1 inch at the rear, ¾ inch at the sides, and 3 inches at the front. Fasten the roof deck to the roof cleats with two pairs of 1¾-inch screws driven through the pilot holes.

Apply a wavy bead of construction adhesive to the top face of the roof deck. Place the roofing metal onto the adhesive so the lip of the roofing is flush against the back side of the rear roof trim. Let the adhesive set up long enough so that the roofing does not move.

Apply wood glue to the front and side edges of the roof deck. Fit the front and side roof-trim pieces over the glued edges, and clamp them in place. Fasten the trim to the roof deck with three 1¼-inch finish nails driven through the trim and into the edges of the roof deck. Let the glue dry overnight.

Apply a smooth, even bead of silicone caulk along the sides and front of the roofing to seal the joint between the trim and the roofing metal. Smooth the caulk with your finger, then let it dry overnight (photo 9).

MOUNTING YOUR MINI SHED TO A POST

Cut a 2 × 4 block to fit between the roof and the bottom of the box, mitering the top end at 5 degrees to match the roof slope. Mount the block to the side panel of the box with glue and 1¾-inch screws driven through the inside of the box. Mount the shed to the post with two ¼ × 5-inch lag screws driven through the inside of the box, through the block, and into the post.

Build and Hang the Door

Cut a ½ × ½-inch rabbet along one edge of the 1 × 1½-inch pine board. Cut the doorframe sides and top and bottom, mitering their ends at 45 degrees. Dry-assemble (no glue) the doorframe and clamp it both directions. Drill a countersunk pilot hole at each corner of the frame, angling the hole through the top/bottom piece and into the side piece. Make sure the hole does not interfere with the rabbet on either piece.

Note: If you don't want to rabbet the doorframe pieces, you can cut the glazing a little larger and mount it to the back side of the assembled frame (see Making Doors with [or without] Rabbets on page 34).

Unclamp the frame pieces, apply glue to the ends of each piece, and assemble the frame with a 2¼ wood screw at each joint.

Cut the glazing stops from ⅜ × ⅜-inch stock, mitering both ends at 45 degrees. Measure the width and height of the doorframe opening, measuring from rabbet to rabbet. Subtract ⅛ inch from each dimension, then cut the door

glazing to this size (see Cutting and Drilling Plastic Glazing on page 35). You will install the glazing after painting or staining the project.

Mount the door hinges to the doorframe using the provided screws. The jamb-side half of the hinge should be aligned with the top/bottom edge of the doorframe. Hang the door so its bottom edge is flush with the bottom of the box, driving the hinge screws into the front corner trim (photo 10). You can hang the door from either side, depending on which way you want the door to swing.

Complete the Project

Remove the door and hinges. Finish the project as desired (see Painting & Staining on pages 39–42 for finishing tips). When the finish is completely dry, fit the glazing into the rabbets of the doorframe and secure it with the glazing stops, nailed at each end and in the center with a ¾-inch finish nail. Rehang the door as before.

Learn how to register your Little Free Library on page 156.

Rustic Shed

The Rustic Shed is a fun-to-build project that's perfect for a light stain or a clear coat finish that shows off its natural wood details. The project starts with a standard plywood box that includes a removable shelf and a roof panel that is inset into the top of the box. Once the box is built, you cover its sides, back, and top with a decorative skin of rustic cedar plywood or solid pine boards. Then, it's time for the trim—the sides, back, and roof all get strips of rough-cut cedar or pine that adds the look of traditional board-and-batten siding.

Part of what makes this structure fun to build is choosing the materials. While the interior box works best with ordinary plywood, the decorative panels and trim can be almost any material you like. As shown here, the panels are made with ⅜-inch cedar plywood. Another good option is edge-glued solid cedar or pine, which is commonly sold at lumberyards and home centers in 16-inch-, 24-inch-, and 48-inch-wide planks and panels. The trim is rough-sawn cedar. If you have trouble finding the trim pieces in the specified sizes, you can easily substitute with whatever's available in your area. Or perhaps you might use some old salvaged material you've been saving, or even try something like tobacco lath (see Tobacco Barn on page 91).

The same goes for the panels. This is a great opportunity to use some old barn boards or pallet wood or even tongue-and-groove siding. The idea behind the plywood box is that it keeps the interior of the structure clean and dry even if the decorative skin on the outside isn't exactly watertight or airtight. That means you can leave knotholes, rough edges, and other characterful flaws as they are and not worry about the weather getting inside.

INSTRUCTIONS

Cut the Plywood Parts

Cut the side panels, back panel, base, top, shelf, and shelf supports to size using a circular saw or jigsaw. Note that the side panels are 22 inches long on one side edge and 20 inches long on the other side edge. Cut the top panel with a 9-degree bevel on the front and rear edges so the bevels are parallel to each other (photo 1). The side edges of the top are square-cut.

1. Cut the front and rear edges of the plywood top at 9° so the panel will follow the roof slope and the edges will fit flush against the front and back panels. 2. The back panel fits over the sides and base; the top fits between the sides and up against the back panel. 3. Notch the side edge of the front panel so the hinges will install flush with the panel edge.

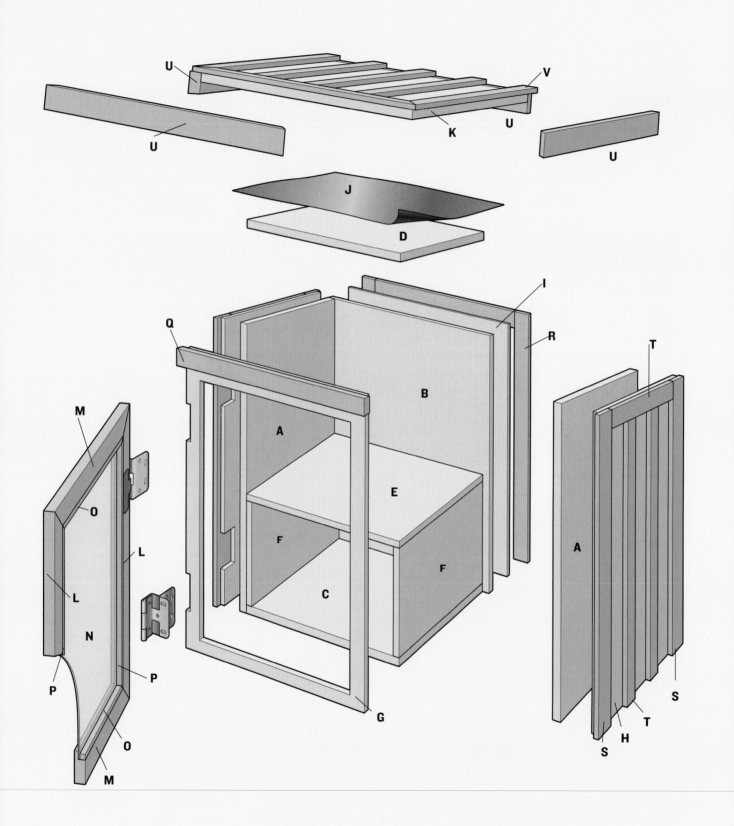

TOOLS & MATERIALS

Circular saw
Jigsaw
Clamps
Drill-driver
Pilot-countersink bit
Screwdriver bit
⅜" drill bit
Utility knife
Wood chisel
Router and ½" rabbeting bit (optional)
Miter saw or miter box
Hammer
Nail set
4 × 4' sheet of ⅝" plywood
2 × 4' piece of ½" plywood
4 × 8' sheet of ⅜" cedar plywood siding
¾ × 20 × 19" edge-glued cedar or pine board
1 × 3" (nominal) × 8' pine
⅜ × ⅜ × 96" cedar
(4) ⅜ × 1 5/16 × 96" cedar
⅝ × 1⅝ × 96" cedar
⅜ × 2 × 96" cedar
17½ × 18½" 6-mil plastic sheeting
(4) 3" wood screws
(36) 1⅝" trim screws
(6) 1¼" wood screws
(3) ⅞" wood screws
(20) ¾" wood screws
(116) 1¼" finish nails
(2) exterior offset hinges (for ¾" doorframe) with screws
Waterproof wood glue
Eye and ear protection
Work gloves

CUTTING LIST

KEY	PART	DIMENSIONS	PCS.	MATERIAL
A	Side panel	⅝ × 12 15/16 × 22"	2	Plywood
B	Back panel	⅝ × 15⅜ × 20"	1	Plywood
C	Base	⅝ × 12 15/16 × 14 3/16"	1	Plywood
D	Top	⅝ × 13⅛ × 14 3/16"	1	Plywood
E	Shelf	⅝ × 12 13/16 × 14⅛"	1	Plywood
F	Shelf support	½ × 12 13/16 × 7 15/16"	2	Plywood
G	Front panel	½ × 22" × cut to fit	1	Plywood
H	Siding—sidewall	⅜ × 13⅞ × 22"	2	Plywood siding
I	Siding—back wall	⅜ × 15⅜ × 19 15/16"	1	Plywood siding
J	Roof underlayment	17½ × 18½"	1	Plastic sheeting
K	Roof	¾ × 19 5/16 × 18½"	1	Edge-glued cedar
L	Doorframe—sides	¾ × 2¼ × 20¾"	2	Pine
M	Doorframe—top/bottom	¾ × 2¼ × 16¾"	2	Pine
N	Door glazing	⅛ × 13 3/16 × 17 3/16"	1	Acrylic glazing
O	Glazing stop—top/bottom	⅜ × ⅜" × cut to fit	2	Cedar
P	Glazing stop—side	⅜ × ⅜" × cut to fit	2	Cedar
Q	Door-header trim	¾ × 1⅛" × cut to fit	1	Cedar
R	Trim—back wall	⅜ × 1 5/16" × cut to fit	6	Cedar
S	Trim—sidewall, outer	⅜ × 2" × cut to fit	4	Cedar
T	Trim—sidewall, inner	⅜ × 1 5/16" × cut to fit	6	Cedar
U	Trim—roof edge	⅝ × 1⅝" × cut to fit	4	Cedar
V	Trim—rooftop	⅜ × 1 5/16" × cut to fit	6	Cedar

Assemble the Plywood Box

The initial box assembly includes the sides (with shelf supports), back, base, and top. Later, you will cut the front panel to fit over the box and the outer siding material. The shelf is removable and simply rests on the shelf supports.

Apply glue to one side face of each shelf support. Place a support against the inside face of one side panel so both pieces are flush at the side and bottom edges. Clamp the parts together (or weight them down with heavy weights). Let the glue dry for at least 1 hour before removing the clamps.

Apply glue to the side and rear edges of the base and to the rear edges of the side panels. Fit the back against the rear edge of the base, then fit the side panels over the side edges of the base and up against the back panel. Make sure all pieces are flush at the bottom and fasten along each edge with three 1⅝-inch trim screws.

Glue the side and rear edges of the top and fit it between the side and back panels so all pieces are flush at the top. Fasten the top with three 1⅝-inch trim screws along each edge (photo 2).

Cut the Front Panel

Measure the width across the front of the box assembly. To this dimension, add twice the thickness of your siding material. For example, if your box is 15⅜ inches wide and your siding material is ⅜ inch thick, the total width dimension is 16⅛ inches (15⅜ inches + ¾ inch = 16⅛ inches). Cut the front panel to size using your total width dimension and 22 inches for the height.

To mark the door cutout, draw a 13¹¹⁄₁₆ × 19¹⁄₁₆-inch rectangle onto the front panel starting ⅞ inch up from the bottom edge and centering the rectangle side to side. Drill a ⅜-inch starter hole (see Making Curves and Interior Cutouts on page 32) on the inside of each corner of the rectangle and complete the cutout with a jigsaw.

Cut a ⅜-inch-deep × 2¾-inch-wide notch into one of the side edges of the front panel using a jigsaw (photo 3). These notches create a recess for the hinges, so adjust the size of the notches according to your hinges, as needed. You can locate the hinges at either side of the structure, based on which way you'd like the door to swing.

4. Using a jigsaw, cut out a mortise for each hinge leaf so the hinges mount flush (or slightly below flush) with the face of the siding. 5. Fasten the side-panel siding along the edges, placing the screws where they will be covered by trim later. 6. The roofing underlayment helps prevent leaks if any moisture gets through the roof material. 7. Cut the acrylic door glazing to size with a jigsaw and metal- or plastic-cutting blade. 8. Space the inner vertical pieces evenly between the outside trims on the back wall.

Install the Front Panel

Apply glue to the front edges of the side panels, base, and top and set the front panel over the glued edges so the bottom of the front panel is flush with the bottom of the base and the front panel overhangs the side panels equally on both sides. Fasten the front panel to each box panel with three 1⅝-inch trim screws.

Prepare the Siding

Cut the siding pieces for the sides and rear of the structure. The sides have an angled top edge that follows the roof slope. The front side is 22 inches, and the rear side is 19¾ inches. **Note:** The siding at the sidewalls will overlap the siding at the back; if necessary, adjust the width of your sidewall siding to accommodate the thickness of the siding material on the back panel.

Cut notches for the hinges on the side where the door will hang. Position the siding against the side of the box, butted against the back face of the front panel and flush at the top. Transfer the locations of the hinge notches from the front panel to the siding. Place a hinge at each set of marks and trace around the hinge leaf to draw the notch cutouts. Cut the notches with a jigsaw (photo 4).

Install the Siding

Apply a wavy bead of glue to the inside face of the back-panel siding. Place the siding against the back of the box so all edges are flush. Fasten the siding to the back panel with ¾-inch screws. (**Note:** Use shorter screws if your siding is thinner than ⅜ inch.) Use four evenly spaced screws along the top of the siding, ¾ inch from the top edge. Use four screws along the bottom, ⅜ inch from the bottom edge.

Apply glue to each side panel siding piece, and fit it against the side of the box so it butts against the front panel and overlaps the edges of the back panel siding. Fasten each side with four screws along each edge. At the bottom of the siding, space the interior screws 5 inches from the front and rear side edges; this ensures the screw heads will be covered by the wall trim (photo 5).

Install the Roof

Cut the roof panel to size. Cut the roof underlayment to size using a utility knife or scissors. Lay the underlayment onto the top of the box so it overhangs about 1 inch at all sides (photo 6).

Place the roof on top of the underlayment so it overhangs the box about 1¼ inches at the back, 2⅜ inches at the front, and equally on both sides. Fasten the roof to the plywood top of the box with three pairs of 1¼-inch screws (use shorter screws if your roof material is thinner than ¾ inch). Drive one pair 5 inches from each side edge and 3 inches and 13½ inches from the rear edge of the roof. Drive the third pair centered side to side on the roof, 3 inches and 13½ inches from the rear edge. The screws will be covered by the roof trim.

Build the Doorframe

Rip-cut an 8-foot 1 × 3 board to width at 2³⁄₁₆ inches. Cut a ½ × ½-inch rabbet along at least 82 inches of the board (see Making Doors with [or without] Rabbets on page 34 for help with cutting rabbets). Using the rabbeted section of the board, cut the doorframe sides and top and bottom, mitering their ends at 45 degrees.

Assemble the doorframe and clamp it both directions. Drill a pilot hole at each corner of the frame, angling the hole through the top/bottom piece and into the side piece. Make sure the hole does not interfere with the rabbet on either piece.

Unclamp the frame pieces, apply glue to the end of each piece, and assemble the frame with a 3-inch wood screw at each joint.

Cut the glazing stops from ⅜ × ⅜-inch stock, mitering both ends at 45 degrees. Measure the width and height of the doorframe opening, measuring from rabbet to rabbet. Subtract ⅛ inch from each dimension, then cut the door glazing to this size (see Cutting and Drilling Plastic Glazing on page 35) (photo 7). You will install the glazing after the wood parts are finished and before hanging the door. However, if you'd like, you can hang the door now for a dry run (see Dry-Assemble the Shed on page 47), then remove the door and hinges for the finishing process.

9. Install all the side-trim pieces except the vertical piece that will cover the door hinges. 10. Fit the flat trim to the rooftop. Notice, also, how the roof grain runs from side to side and the outer roof-top trim is installed about ⅛" away from the outsides of the edge trim to create a decorative reveal. 11. Clamp one of the hinges to the door while screwing the other hinge to the doorframe.

Finish the Wood

Apply the finish of your choice to the box structure, the doorframe (and glazing stops), and the trim material. You can use different finishes for the box, door, and trim, if desired. For example, it looks good to use a light-colored stain or clear coat on the box and door and add some contrast with a darker color of stain for the trim. Prefinishing the parts saves time and helps protect the wood from moisture that may get behind the trim.

The only piece that needs cutting at this stage is the door-header trim: using a scrap piece of siding material, cut a strip that is 1⅛ inch wide so that the top edge is beveled at 9 degrees. Then, cut the piece to length at 17¹⁄₁₆ inches or as needed to match the width of the front panel. Finish the header trim to match the other trim pieces.

Apply the Back-Wall Trim

The back wall gets six pieces of trim, all with square ends. Cut the two outside vertical pieces so they extend from the bottom of the base to the roof. Position each piece against the back siding so it is flush with the outside face of the side-panel siding and fasten it with four 1¼-inch finish nails.

Cut the horizontal trim across the top to fit snugly between the two vertical trims and up against the roof. Fasten it with three 1¼-inch finish nails.

Cut the three remaining vertical-trim pieces to extend from the base to the horizontal trim. Install them evenly spaced between the two outer vertical trims using four nails each (photo 8).

Apply the Sidewall Trim

Each sidewall has two outer vertical trims, a horizontal (angled) trim at the top, and two inner vertical trims. The vertical pieces are square-cut at the bottom and mitered at 9 degrees at the top. The horizontal trim is mitered at both ends at 9 degrees.

Cut the vertical trim at the rear side to cover the back wall trim at the corner and extend to the roof, mitering the top end at 9 degrees. Install it with four finish nails. Cut the vertical trim at the front side to cover the edge of the front panel and extend to the roof and install with four nails.

Note: Don't nail the vertical trim that will cover the hinges. Just clamp it in place for now; you will install it after hanging the door.

Cut the horizontal trim to fit between the vertical trims and install it with three nails. Cut the two inner vertical trims so they are evenly spaced between the two outer trims and install them with four nails each (photo 9). Remove the clamped trim piece and set it aside for installing later.

Install the Door-Header Trim

The header trim installs with ⅞-inch screws instead of finish nails. Fit the header trim with its beveled edge up against the roof and its ends flush with the side edges of the front panel. Reach inside the box and drive three screws through the front panel and into the trim.

Apply the Roof Trim

The roof gets four pieces of ⅝-inch-thick trim wrapping the outside edges. Then, it gets three pieces of ⅜-inch-thick "rooftop" trim along the side and top edges (partially overlapping the ⅝-inch trim) plus three more strips spaced evenly across the top surface of the roof.

Cut the edge piece for the back edge with square ends to match the width of the roof. Fit it flush to the face and side edges of the roof panel and nail it with four 1¼-inch finish nails. Cut the two side edge pieces so they completely overlap the rear edge piece and end with a 45-degree miter at the front corner of the roof. Install them flush with the rooftop with four nails each.

Cut and install the front edge piece with a 45-degree miter at both ends to meet the side pieces at the corners.

Make short pencil marks at the ends of the front and side trims, parallel to and ⅛ inch from the outside of the trim. This is where you will install the outer pieces of the rooftop trim to create a decorative lip—called a reveal—along the sides and front of the roof.

Cut the three outer-rooftop trims so they are mitered at 45 degrees at the front corners and flush with the edge trims at the back of the roof (photo 10). Install the pieces so their outside edges are on the marked lines, creating a ⅛-inch reveal, nailing each piece with four nails.

Cut the three interior-rooftop pieces to run from the front trim to the back face of the back edge trim. Space them evenly across the rooftop and nail each with four nails.

Hang the Door

Install the glazing before hanging the door. Fit the glazing into the rabbets of the doorframe and secure it with the glazing stops, nailed at each end and in the center with a 1¼-inch finish nail.

The door is hung with offset-style hinges (sometimes called institutional hinges) that mount into the notches you cut into the sidewall siding. Mount the hinges to the siding using the provided screws. The hinge leaf that will mount to the back of the door should be flat against the front face of the front panel when the hinge is in the closed position.

Position the door on the hinges so its bottom edge is flush with the bottom of the front panel. Secure the door to one of the hinges with a clamp. Screw the other hinge to the inside face of the doorframe with the provided screws (photo 11). Remove the clamp and fasten the other hinge to the door.

Install the Final Trim Piece

Fit the outer vertical trim piece (the one you had set aside) over the hinges on the sidewall so the trim is flush with the front panel. Fasten the trim with three 1¼-inch finish nails.

Learn how to register your Little Free Library on page 156.

Flower Box

If you've ever dreamed of having a house or a potting shed with a grass roof, this little cultivatable structure is a good place to start. It's a simple plywood cube with a shallow cavity in the top that holds a garden tray—or, in this case, a deep cake pan—where all the gardening happens. The tray lifts right out, so you can bring your plants inside for cold nights or to a convenient location for tending. The box has its own plywood roof that stays watertight with or without the tray in place.

This easy building project starts with finding just the right tray or pan for your rooftop garden. It must be fully enclosed, with no holes or vents, and it must be strong enough to hold several pounds of soil, plants, and water (a seedling tray isn't strong enough). The tray also should have a continuous lip along the top—this rests on the top edges of the box to support the tray. A depth of about 3 inches is ideal, but a little deeper or shallower is okay. This depth works well for small flowers, like pansies or Johnny-jump-ups, as well as wheatgrass and other shallow-root decorative plants.

The tray shown here is a 16-inch-square, 3-inch-deep aluminum cake pan, and the box is just under 18 inches all around. You can adjust the dimensions of your box to fit any tray. Just measure the width of the tray (under the lip) and build the box so the tray basin easily slips into the cavity at the top of the box. The lip of the tray will rest on the box's edges. You can also adjust the height of the box to roughly match the width and depth, to form a cube shape.

An eye-catching structure like this just begs for a colorful paint job. To make the box look nice, you'll learn how to cover the exposed plywood edges with an epoxy wood filler (Bondo is one well-known brand) or other exterior wood filler so the entire box has a smooth, seamless look. And you can't go wrong with a garden-themed door handle or other custom decoration.

INSTRUCTIONS
Cut the Plywood Parts
Cut the side panels, front panel, back panel, top, and base to size using a circular saw or jigsaw. Remember, you can alter the dimensions of these pieces to accommodate the tray you're using. The tray should fit into the top of the box with just ⅛ inch to ¼ inch of wiggle room.

1. Measure the door opening in the front panel and cut the door to fit, leaving space for the hinges and a small gap along the door edges. 2. Drill the drainage holes through the back panel, angling them slightly downward from the inside to the outside.

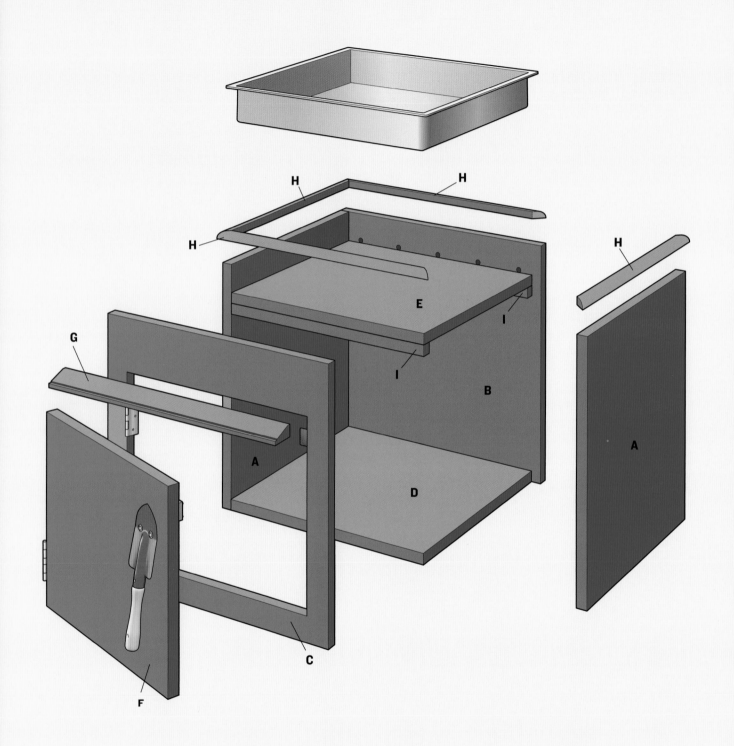

TOOLS & MATERIALS

Circular saw (optional)
Jigsaw
Drill-driver
Drill bit (⅜")
Piloted bit for hinge screws
Pilot-countersink bit
Screwdriver bit
Hammer
Miter saw or miter box
Nail set
Putty knife or plastic spreader

Caulking gun
4 × 8' sheet of ¾" plywood
½ × ¾ × 96" pine base shoe molding
¹¹⁄₁₆ × 1⅝ × 18" pine drip cap molding
16 × 16 × 3" cake pan or tray (aluminum, stainless steel, or plastic)
(36) 1¾" wood screws
(34) 1¼" finish nails
(5) 1" finish nails

Waterproof wood glue
Exterior epoxy wood filler
80- and 180-grit sandpaper
Paintable exterior caulk
(2) No-mortise stainless steel cabinet hinges with screws
Magnetic door catch for inset cabinet doors
Garen hand trowel
Eye and ear protection
Work gloves

CUTTING LIST

KEY	PART	DIMENSIONS	PCS.	MATERIAL
A	Side panel	¾ × 16¼ × 17¼"	2	Plywood
B	Back panel	¾ × 17¾ × 17¼"	1	Plywood
C	Front panel	¾ × 17¾ × 17¼"	1	Plywood
D	Base	¾ × 16¼ × 16¼"	1	Plywood
E	Top	¾ × 16¼ × 16¼"	1	Plywood
F	Door	¾ × 14¼ × 11⅞"	1	Plywood
G	Drip cap	¹¹⁄₁₆ × 1⅝ × 17¾"	1	Drip cap molding
H	Top trim	½ × ¾ × 17¾"	4	Base shoe molding
I	Cleat	¾ × ¾ × 16¼"	2	Plywood

Cut the Door Opening and Door

Mark a rectangle on the back side of the front panel so its edges are 1⅝ inches from the side and bottom edges and 3½ inches from the top edge. Drill a ⅜-inch-diameter starter hole (see Making Curves and Interior Cutouts on page 32) at each corner of the rectangle, just inside the marked lines. Use the jigsaw to cut between the starter holes to complete the cutout for the door opening.

Measure the width and height of the door opening (photo 1). Also measure the thickness of one of the door hinges when it is closed flat. Add ⅛ inch to the hinge thickness and subtract the result from the width of the door opening; this is the final door width. Subtract ¼ inch from the height of the door opening; this is the height of the door. For example, if the door opening is 14½ inches wide × 12⅛ inches tall, and the hinge is ⅛ inch thick, the door dimensions are:

width: 14½ inches - ⅛ inch - ⅛ inch = 14¼ inches
height: 12⅛ inches - ¼ inch = 11⅞ inches

Cut the door to size.

Add the Cleats

Cut two strips of plywood to about ¾ inch wide and no longer than 16¼ inches (they can be shorter) to make the cleats. Draw two parallel lines across the inside face of the front panel, 2¾ inches and 3½ inches down from, and parallel to, the top edge. Draw two similar lines on the back panel, 3 inches and 3¾ inches from the top edge.

3. Glue and nail the drip cap to the front panel, nailing into the lip between the top edge and the angled plane of the drip cap. 4. Cap the top edges of the box with base shoe molding so the rounded side of the molding faces up and the flat ½" edge faces in.

Apply glue to one face of one of the cleats and position it on the front panel so its top edge is on the lower line and it is centered side to side. Then fasten the cleat with three 1¼-inch finish nails. Do the same to install the remaining cleat on the back panel.

Drill the Drainage Holes

The back panel gets five ⅜-inch-diameter drainage holes to let water escape from the top cavity. Water will fall into the cavity only if the tray is not in place (assuming that your planting tray doesn't have its own drainage holes).

Make marks for the five holes on the inside face of the back panel, along the upper line, above the cleat. Make one mark 1 inch from each corner, then mark about every 3½ inches in between. Clamp the back panel over a sacrificial surface to prevent tearout on the backside of the plywood.

Drill a ⅜-inch hole at each mark, drilling from the inside of the back panel so the bottom of the hole just touches the line. Hold the drill so the bit makes a slight downward angle from the inside to the outside of the back panel (photo 2).

Assemble the Box

Apply glue to the side edges of the base. Fit the side panels over the sides of the base so the pieces are flush at the front, rear, and bottom. Drive three 1¾-inch screws through each side panel and into the edge of the base.

Glue the rear edges of the side panels and base. Fit the back panel over the assembly so all pieces are flush on the outside. Fasten the back to the sides and base with three 1¾-inch screws along each edge. Install the front panel in the same way.

Check the fit of the top panel: it should fit snugly into the open top of the box. If necessary, sand the edges of the top panel so it will fit, but do not push into the box.

Apply a bead of glue between the upper line and the cleat on both the front and back panels. Fit the top panel into the box and tap it down carefully with a hammer or mallet until it rests on the cleats. It will slope down ¼ inch from front to back (for drainage). Let the glue dry overnight.

Install the Drip Cap

Cut the drip cap to length with a miter saw, miter box, or jigsaw. Place the box on its back and mark a horizontal line ½ inch above the top of the door opening on the front panel. Apply glue to the rear edge of the drip cap and position the cap on the front panel so its bottom edge is on the marked line and its ends are flush with the sides of the box. Fasten the drip cap to the front panel with four evenly spaced 1-inch finish nails. Drive the nails at a slight downward angle through the lip at the top of the drip edge (photo 4). Set the nails slightly below the surface with a nail set (see Screwing and Nailing in Wood on page 33).

Add the Top Trim

Cut the top trim to length, mitering both ends of each piece at 45 degrees using a miter saw or miter box; lay the trim on its ¾-inch-wide face for cutting.

Apply glue to the ¾-inch face of the trim and fit the pieces along the top edges of the box so the tapered "nose" of the trim is flush with the outside faces of the box and the mitered ends meet at the corners (photo 5). Fasten each piece of trim with four 1¼-inch finish nails.

Prepare the Box for Finishing

If you'd like to paint your project, prepare it by filling and smoothing all of the exposed plywood edges with wood filler and caulking inside the top cavity and along the top of the drip cap. All of the filler and caulk will be hidden by the paint. If you prefer to stain or clear coat your project, skip the filler (it doesn't look like wood), and caulk the top and drip cap with clear caulk after you've applied the wood finish.

If you're painting the box, mix the wood filler according to the manufacturer's directions. Epoxy wood fillers are mixed by combining the filler base with a hardener and mixing thoroughly for about 2 minutes. Mix a small amount at a time and apply it quickly, as the filler sets up in only a few minutes.

Once the filler is mixed, apply it to the plywood edges of the box and door panel using a wide putty knife or a plastic spreader (photo 6). Press the filler into any voids in the edges, then smooth the surface flat. The smoother and flatter it is, the less sanding you'll need to do later. Also cover all screw and nail heads so the holes are completely filled. Let the filler harden as directed (it may take only 10 to 15 minutes).

Sand the hardened filler flat with 80-grit sandpaper, focusing on high spots and rough areas. Final-sand the filler and bare plywood surfaces with 180-grit sandpaper so the filler is smoothly feathered into the wood areas.

Complete the Project

Apply paintable exterior caulk along the edges inside the top cavity of the box, including the vertical corners where the sides and front/rear panels meet. Also caulk along the top edge of the drip cap to seal it against the front panel. Let the caulk cure as directed by the manufacturer.

Prime and paint the entire box and door, as desired (see Painting & Staining on page 39 for painting tips).

Mount the hinges to either side edge of the door, depending on which way you'd like the door to swing, using the provided screws. The laminated edges of plywood aren't great for holding screws; it helps to drill small pilot holes for the screws and drive the screws carefully to prevent stripping them in wood layers.

Mount the door to the edge of the door cutout, again using pilot holes and the provided screws. Make sure the door is centered in the opening so there is an equal gap at the top and bottom.

Install a magnetic door catch on the inside faces of the door and front panel (photo 7). The catch bracket serves as a doorstop, and the magnet gently holds the door closed.

Tip: Add a door handle of your choice. To mount a garden trowel or similar custom piece, you can use long, skinny machine bolts with a washer and nut on the back side of the item and on both sides of the door.

5. Press the wood filler into the plywood edges to fill all voids and gaps, then smooth the filler with the putty knife. **6.** Mount the door-catch bracket to the interior side of the front panel and mount the magnet unit to the inside of the door.

Learn how to register your Little Free Library on page 156.

Two-Story Shed

The Two-Story Shed is one of the largest of the Little Free Library designs. Measuring in at 21 inches wide × 23½ inches tall × 19 inches deep, it has plenty of room inside for a shelf (or you can leave out the shelf in favor of an extra-tall interior space). The sides, back, base, and shelf are made with ¾-inch plywood, giving this tall structure a little extra heft. A metal roof tops it off with a professional touch.

But perhaps the best feature of this structure is the big 21 × 15-inch door that provides a nearly full view of the roomy interior. The door isn't just large and invitingly see-through; it's also well-made, with a solid pine frame with mitered (as in a picture frame) corners that give it strength and a finished look.

The doorframe is a little trickier to build than some other door designs, as it requires cutting a rabbet (L-shaped notch) along one full edge of each piece. The structural trim pieces at both sides of the door also have rabbets. But if you're up for some careful layout and cutting with a circular saw—or, better yet, a router or a tablesaw, if you have access to either one—you'll get the satisfaction of learning how to create a classic woodworking detail. A router also comes in handy for cutting the dadoes (grooves) in the sidewalls to hold the shelf in place.

INSTRUCTIONS

Cut the Plywood Parts

Cut all the plywood parts to the dimensions given in the cutting list (page 77). There are seven parts total. Note that the side and back panels, base, and shelf are cut from ¾-inch plywood; the front panel is ½-inch plywood; and the roof deck is ¼-inch plywood.

To lay out the angled top edge of each side panel, draw a 13 × 22⁵⁄₁₆-inch rectangle. Measure up one side edge and mark it at 18¾ inches. Draw a line from this mark to the top corner on the other side of the piece to create the angle (photo 1).

Cut the Shelf Dadoes

The dadoes are ¼-inch-deep grooves cut into the interior faces of the side panels to hold the shelf. You can cut them with a circular saw or a router and a straight router bit. The shelf is ¾-inch plywood, which actually measures slightly thinner, typically ²³⁄₃₂ inch, so this is the width to make the dadoes. If you have a ²³⁄₃₂-inch router bit, you can mill each dado with one pass. (**Tip:** To find the exact thickness of your plywood, you can measure the material itself or trace along both faces of a scrap piece of the plywood and measure between the marks.)

1. The side panels have angled top edges to create the roof slope.
2. Use a straightedge guide to cut the bottom edge of the dado with a circular saw or a router. 3. Using a chisel, clean out the remaining wood left by the circular saw in the dado.

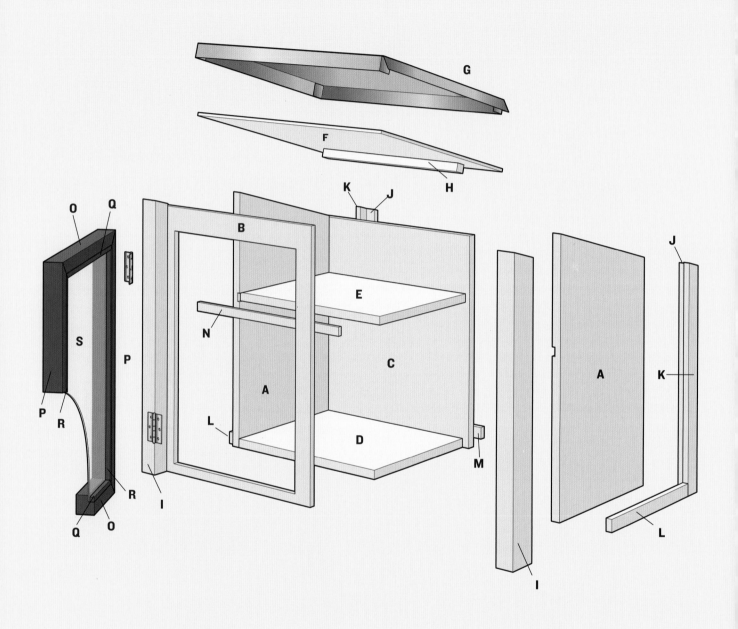

TOOLS & MATERIALS

Circular saw
Straightedge
Router (optional)
Straight and ½" rabbeting router bits
 (optional)
Clamps
Chisel
Jigsaw with wood- and metal- or
 plastic-cutting blades
Drill-driver
Drill bits (⅟₁₆", ⅛", ³⁄₁₆", ½")
Pilot-countersink bit
#2 Phillips screwdriver bit
Hex-head driver bit
Miter saw

Hammer
Nail set (optional)
Aviation snips
Rivet gun
48 × 48" piece of ¾" plywood
24 × 24" piece of ½" plywood
24 × 24" piece of ¼" plywood
24 × 24" piece of 26-gauge
 galvanized steel or aluminum sheet
 metal
¾ × 1 × 16" pine
2 × 3" (nominal) × 8' pine
½ × 1 × 84" pine
½ × 1½ × 38" pine
⅜ × ¾ × 16¼" pine

2 × 2" (nominal) × 8' pine
⅜ × ⅜ × 64" pine
⅛ × 18 × 24" acrylic glazing
(2) exterior door hinges with screws
Waterproof wood glue
(6) 2½" deck screws
(24) 1⅝" deck screws
(31) 1" finish or trim nails
(4) ⅛" aluminum pop rivets
(4) 1½" gasketed metal roofing
 screws
Wood finishing supplies (as needed)
Eye and ear protection
Work gloves

CUTTING LIST

KEY	PART	DIMENSIONS	PCS.	MATERIAL
A	Side panel	13 × 22⁵⁄₁₆"	2	¾" plywood
B	Front panel	17⅛ × 22¼"	1	½" plywood
C	Back panel	17⅛ × 18⅝"	1	¾" plywood
D	Base	15¾ × 13"	1	¾" plywood
E	Shelf	16¼ × 12⅝"	1	¾" plywood
F	Roof deck	21⅛ × 18⅝"	1	¼" plywood
G	Roofing	23⅝ × 21⅛"	1	26-gauge sheet metal
H	Roof cleat	¾ × 1 × 15¹¹⁄₁₆"	1	Pine
I	Front-corner trim	1½ × 2½ × 22¾"	2	Pine
J	Rear-corner trim—back	½ × 1 × 18⁹⁄₁₆"	2	Pine
K	Rear-corner trim—side	½ × 1½ × 18¹³⁄₁₆"	2	Pine
L	Side-bottom trim	½ × 1 × 12⁵⁄₁₆"	2	Pine
M	Back-bottom trim	½ × 1 × 15³⁄₁₆"	1	Pine
N	Shelf molding	⅜ × ¾ × 16¼"	1	Pine
O	Doorframe—top/bottom	1½ × 1½ × 15"	2	Pine
P	Doorframe—side	1½ × 1½ × 21⅛"	2	Pine
Q	Glazing stop—top/bottom	⅜ × ⅜ × 12¹⁵⁄₁₆"	2	Pine
R	Glazing stop—side	⅜ × ⅜ × 19⅛"	2	Pine
S	Door glazing	⅛ × 18 × 24"	1	Acrylic glazing

Otherwise, set up a straightedge guide (see Making Straight Cuts on page 31) to guide your circular saw or router and cut one side of the dado (photo 2). The lower side of the dado is 12¾ inches from the bottom edge of the side panel. Make the first cut, then move the straightedge guide up ²³⁄₃₂ inch (or the measured thickness of your shelf piece) and make a second cut to create the top edge of the dado.

Make several more passes with the circular saw to remove the wood between the first two cuts, then clear out the remaining waste with a sharp chisel (photo 3). If you're using a router and a ⅜-inch or ½-inch bit, you'll need to make only the first two cuts; with a narrower bit, clear out the center of the dado with an extra pass or two.

Cut the Door Opening

The front panel gets a large rectangular cutout for the door opening. This is an interior cutout, and you can make it with a jigsaw (as described here) or a circular saw (if you know how to make plunge cuts).

To make the cutout, mark a 13⅞-inch-wide × 19½-inch-tall rectangle onto the inside face of the front panel. The bottom of the rectangle is ¾ inch from the bottom edge of the panel. The sides of the rectangle are 1⅝ inch from each side of the panel.

Drill a ½-inch-diameter starter hole (see Making Curves and Interior Cutouts on page 32) at each corner of the rectangle. Use the jigsaw to cut between the starter holes to complete the cutout (photo 4).

Prepare the Front-Corner Trim

The two front-corner trim pieces are cut from 2 × 3 lumber, which measures about 1½ × 2½ inches. Each piece gets a ⅞ × 1⅛-inch rabbet cut into one long edge. The rabbets allow the trim to fit over the edges of the front panel and overlap the side panels. Rabbets this deep would be difficult to cut with a router, but you can use a circular saw (or, better yet, a tablesaw, if you have one), using the techniques in Making Doors with [or without] Rabbets on page 34.

Cut the rabbets onto a 2 × 3 that's at least 48 inches long, then cut the two trim pieces to length at 22¾ inches, mitering the top ends of the trim at 15 degrees (see Cutting Trim on page 32 for tips on making angled cuts) (photo 5).

4. Insert the blade of the jigsaw into a starter hole to begin cutting. 5. Cut the corner-trim pieces at 22¾" from the square end to the long point of the 15° angle cut. Rabbet dimensions are ⅞" and 1⅛". 6. Clamp the side panel to the front panel (with pre-attached corner trim), drill pilot holes, and drive screws through the trim and into the side panel. 7. Install the back panel over the edges of the side panels and base. The shelf installs without glue or screws.

Alternatively, you can skip the rabbets and build each trim corner with two pieces of lumber: a 2 × 2 attached to the front panel and overhanging the side edges by ½ inch, plus a piece of ½-inch × 1-inch trim butted up against the 2 × 2 and overlapping the side panel. In this case, install the side trim piece after the box is assembled.

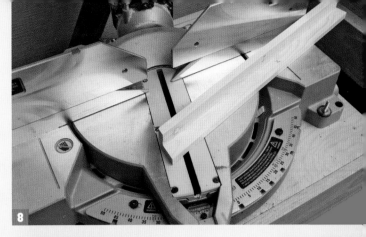

Glue the Front-Corner Trim

Apply wood glue to the ⅞-inch-wide surface of the rabbet on each piece of corner trim. Also glue both side edges of the plywood front panel. Position corner trim along both sides of the front panel so the trim is flush with the bottom edge of the panel; the angle at the top of the trim will extend slightly above the top of the panel. Clamp the pieces in place and let the glue dry for at least 1 hour before removing the clamps.

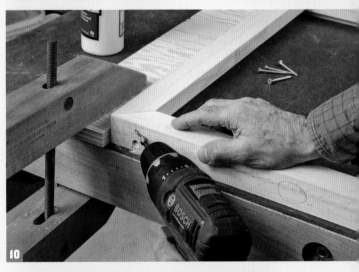

Add the Shelf Molding

Cut the ¾-inch-wide shelf molding to length at 16¼ inches. Apply glue to one face of the molding and clamp it to the front edge of the plywood shelf so the pieces are flush on all sides. Let the glue dry for at least 1 hour before removing the clamps.

Join the Front and Side Panels

Apply glue to the front edge of one of the side panels. Also apply glue to the overhanging portion of the front corner trim. Stand up the front panel and fit the side panel against the front panel and the overlap of the corner trim. The bottom edge of the side panel should be flush with the bottom end of the corner trim.

Clamp the side panel to the front panel, or have a helper hold the pieces together. Drill three evenly spaced pilot holes through the front of the corner trim and into the edge of the side panel (photo 6). Drive 2½-inch deck screws through the trim and into the side panel. Repeat the same process to install the other side panel.

Install the Base, Shelf, and Back Panel

Apply glue to both side edges and the front edge of the base. Fit the base between the side panels so it butts against the

8. Cut the assembled corner trim at a 15° angle, with the side piece against the saw fence (if using a miter saw). Cut corner trim should measure 18¹³⁄₁₆″ from square end to long point. 9. Install all trim flush with the bottom face of the base. The top ends of the trim will be covered by the roof. 10. Drill angled pilot holes on the doorframe using a piloted countersink bit so the screw heads will install about ⅛″ below the wood surface. 11. Test-fit the glazing and stops. The stops will be nailed later to hold the glazing in place.

Apply glue to the rear edges of the side panels and base. Fit the back panel over the glued edges so the side edges of the back are flush with the outsides of the side panels and the bottom edge of the back is flush with the bottom of the base. The top edges of the sides will sit a little higher than the back panel. Drill pilot holes and fasten the back to the sides and base with eight 1⅝-inch screws.

Prepare the Remaining Trim

Each rear-corner trim piece is made up of two pieces of ½-inch-thick pine glued and nailed together. It's easiest to cut the two pieces a little long, assemble them to create the corner angle, then cut the assembly to length as one piece.

Cut the two side and back pieces to a rough length of at least 20 inches. Apply glue to one edge of each back piece and attach it to the face of one side piece with four 1-inch nails to form an L-shaped angle. The two pieces should be flush with each other at one end and flush at the outside of the angle. If you're using finish nails, you have the option of setting the nails with a nail set (see Screwing and Nailing in Wood on page 33).

Cut the assembled angles to length at 18¹³⁄₁₆ inches, making a 15-degree miter cut at the top end. Measure the length from the bottom (square) end of the side piece to the long point at the top end of the side piece (photo 8).

Cut the side-bottom trim to length at 12⁵⁄₁₆ inches. Cut the back-bottom trim to length at 15³⁄₁₆ inches.

Install the Trim

Install all the trim pieces with glue and 1-inch nails. Install the rear-corner trim pieces over the rear corners of the box assembly. Nail through the back piece of the trim and into the plywood back panel with three 1-inch nails. The bottom edges of the trim should be flush with the bottom face of the base.

Place the back-bottom trim between the rear-corner trims so it is flush with the bottom of the base. Nail the trim to the back panel with three 1-inch nails.

Place the side-bottom trim between the front- and rear-corner trim on each side, flush with the base. Secure each piece with three 1-inch nails (photo 9).

Build the Doorframe

Using an 8-foot 2 × 2, cut the rabbet for the doorframe pieces with a circular saw or a tablesaw. The rabbet is ½ inch wide × ½ inch deep. See Making Doors with (or without) Rabbets on page 34 for help with cutting rabbets.

12. Mark the screw holes for the hinges, then drill pilot holes and preinstall the door. 13. Fold the sides of the roof around the edges of the roof deck and secure each corner with a rivet. 14. Drive roofing screws through the roofing and deck and into the side panels. The screws have rubber washers to seal over the screw hole.

front panel and all the pieces are flush at the bottom. Clamp the assembly or have a helper hold the pieces together. Drill three evenly spaced pilot holes and drive 1⅝-inch deck screws through the outsides of the side panels and into the base on each side.

Slide the shelf into the dadoes from the rear of the assembly so the molded edge butts against the front panel.

Cut the doorframe top and bottom pieces to length at 15 inches, mitering each end at 45 degrees. Cut the frame side pieces at 21⅛ inches, also with 45-degree miters. The rabbets run along the short edges of the mitered pieces. Dry-fit the pieces together to so the rabbets form a groove along the inside of the frame. Make sure the joints fit well, and adjust any of the cuts if necessary.

Clamp the pieces together and drill two angled pilot holes at each end of the top and bottom pieces (photo 10). Unclamp and disassemble the frame. Apply glue to the mitered ends of the top and bottom pieces, then reassemble and clamp the frame. Drive 1⅝-inch screws through the pilot holes to secure the frame joints.

Cut the Glazing and Stops

Measure the recess of the doorframe created by the rabbets. Subtract ⅛ inch from the height and width of the recess to provide expansion space for the glazing. Cut the glazing to the resulting dimensions using a jigsaw and metal- or plastic-cutting blade (see Cutting and Drilling Plastic Glazing on page 35 for tips).

Cut the ⅜ × ⅜-inch glazing stops to fit inside the recess, mitering the ends at 45 degrees, as with the doorframe.

Lay the glazing and stops in the recess to make sure everything fits (photo 11). Remove the pieces and set them aside. You will install them after painting (or otherwise finishing) the project.

Hang the Door

You can preinstall the door now, then remove the door and hinges for painting. When the painting is done, it's easy to rehang the door because the screw holes are already in place. Alternatively, you can paint the project before installing the door.

To preinstall the door, lay the front panel face up on your worksurface. Position the doorframe between the front-corner trims so the frame is about ¼ inch from the bottom edge of the front panel and about ⅛ inch from one of the corner trim pieces; this is the side where the hinges will go, and you can choose either side.

Place the hinges about 2 inches from the top and bottom of the doorframe and mark the screw holes with a pencil (photo 12). Remove the hinges and drill ¹⁄₁₆-inch pilot holes (not countersunk) at the marked locations. Install the hinges with the provided screws, then open and close the door to make sure it works smoothly. Remove the door and hinges for finishing.

Construct the Roof

The roof is made of a ¼-inch plywood deck covered with sheet metal. It also has a lumber cleat that helps you position the roof on the box assembly.

Cut the sheet-metal roofing using aviation snips as shown in the diagram on page 38. Fold over the hem edge of each of the four sides and hammer it flat to create a hem (see Working with Sheet Metal on page 37 for tips on working with sheet metal).

Fold the connecting tabs at 90 degrees, then fold each side flap at 90 degrees, using the fold lines as shown in the diagram. It helps to place the roof deck at the center of the metal sheet so the folds will conform to the deck. The connecting tabs go on the insides of the mating side pieces.

Connect each corner by clamping the connecting tab to the mating side flap with a small clamp and drilling a ⅛-inch hole through the tab and flap. Insert a pop rivet from the outside of the roof and secure the rivet with a rivet gun (photo 13). Alternatively, you can fasten the roofing corners with small self-tapping sheet-metal screws.

Cut the roof cleat to length at 15¹¹⁄₁₆ inches. Position the cleat on the underside of the plywood deck so it is 2¼ inches from the rear (21-inch-long) edge of the deck and centered side to side. Mark the cleat's position on the deck with a pencil. Apply glue to one 1-inch-wide face of the cleat and clamp it to the deck on its marks. Let the glue dry for at least 1 hour before removing the clamps.

Complete the Shed

Finish the wood parts of the shed as desired. Place the roof upside down to mark the screw holes for installing the roof. Make four marks, 2⅜ inches from the side edge and 3⅞ inches from the front/back edge of the deck. Place a piece of scrap wood under each hole location and drill a ³⁄₁₆-inch hole through the roof deck and roofing; the scrap wood prevents you from drilling into your worksurface.

Position the roof on the box assembly so the roof cleat fits in between the side panels and is touching the inside face of the back panel. Secure the roof to the side panels with four 1½-inch roofing screws driven through the predrilled holes using a drill and hex-head driver bit (photo 14).

Complete the door installation by placing the glazing in the frame recess, followed by the stops. Secure each stop with two 1-inch nails driven into the doorframe. Hang the door with the hinges.

Learn how to register your Little Free Library on page 156.

Modern Two-Story

The Modern Two-Story is a simple, stylish, and sizable structure with a sheet-metal roof. If you look closely, you'll notice that it looks at lot like the standard Two-Story Shed (page 75), but instead of the roof sloping from front to back, the Modern Two-Story's roof slopes from side to side. The door is on one of the sloping sides and follows the roof. This means that it's not a rectangle, but rather—as any geometry fan will tell you—a trapezoid. (You can crack up your math-nerd friends by calling it a "trapdoor.")

The funky angles of the Modern Two-Story may make it seem harder to build than it really is. In reality, the design starts with a simple plywood box (as with most of the other projects in this book), and most of the trim pieces are square on one end and are miter-cut on the other end. To simplify several of the corner trims, you can glue together flat strips of wood to form L-shaped angles before cutting the pieces to length. Alternatively, if you have a tablesaw, you can cut these pieces from solid lumber and skip the gluing. In any case, it's best to have a power miter saw, or at least a miter box, for the many angled cuts.

The roofing is appropriately sleek and simple for this modern-style structure. It's made with a plywood rectangle topped with a single piece of sheet metal that is bent along one edge. Three L-shaped trim pieces finish it off, leaving the bottom edge open for water to run off to the side.

INSTRUCTIONS

Cut the Plywood Parts

Cut the left side, right side, back, base, shelf supports, shelf, and roof deck to size using a circular saw or jigsaw. All the pieces are rectangular except for the back, which has an angled top edge. To lay out the back panel, mark it as a $17^{15}/_{16} \times 22^{3}/_{16}$-inch rectangle, then measure down $2^{9}/_{16}$ inches from one top corner and make a mark. Draw a line from the mark to the opposing top corner. Cut along the angled line.

Assemble the Plywood Box

Cut the doorsill to length. Apply glue to one of its faces and position it against one long edge of the plywood base so it is $1^{7}/_{8}$ inches from each corner and is flush with the top face of the base. Clamp the sill in place and let the glue dry. The edge with the sill is the front of the base.

1. The side panels fit over the edges of the base and back panel. 2. Notch the bottom end of each doorpost, cutting into the back face and bottom end of the post. 3. The post-header assembly fits between the side panels and serves as the front side of the structure.

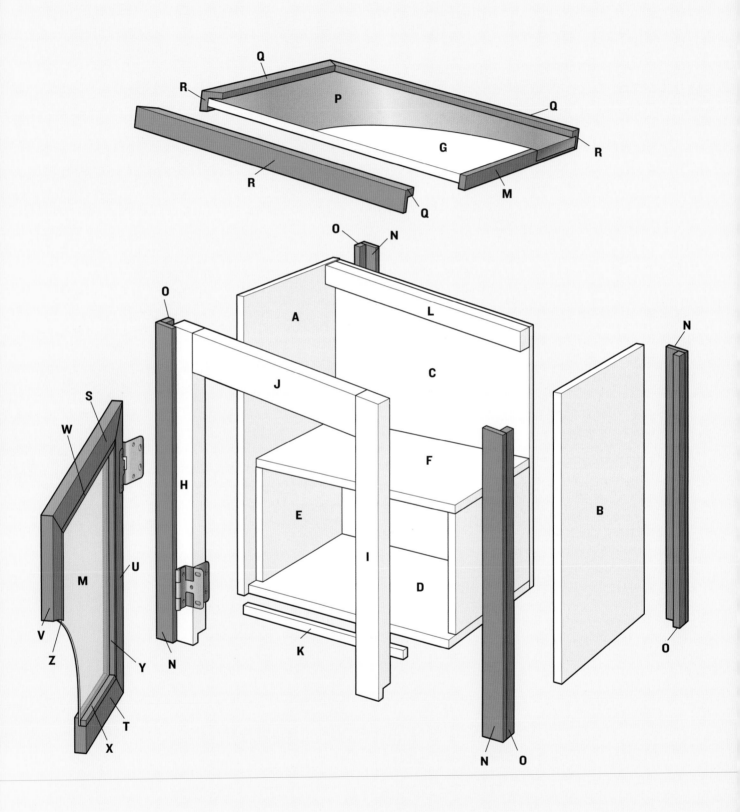

TOOLS & MATERIALS

Circular saw or jigsaw
Clamps
Straightedge guide
Miter saw or miter box
Drill-driver
Pilot-countersink bit
Screwdriver bit
Hammer
Nail set
Aviation snips
Flat-nose pliers
Caulking gun

Router and ½" rabbeting bit (optional)
4 × 8' sheet of ⅝" plywood
2 × 4" (nominal) × 8' pine
9⁄16 × 9⁄16 × 15" pine
(2) ½ × 1 × 96" pine
(2) ½ × 1½ × 96" pine
1 × 3 (nominal) × 8' pine
⅜ × ⅜ × 72" pine
24 × 24" piece of 26-gauge galvanized
  steel or aluminum sheet metal
⅛ × 12 × 16" acrylic glazing
(12) 3" wood screws

(12) 1¾" wood screws
(18) 1⅝" trim screws
(8) 1" wood screws
(15) 1¼" finish nails
(17) 1" finish nails
(2) exterior offset hinges (for ¾"
  doorframe) with screws
Waterproof wood glue
Construction adhesive
Clear exterior silicone caulk
Eye and ear protection
Work gloves

CUTTING LIST

KEY	PART	DIMENSIONS	PCS.	MATERIAL
A	Left side	⅝ × 13⅝ × 22¼"	1	Plywood
B	Right side	⅝ × 13⅝ × 19⁹⁄16"	1	Plywood
C	Back panel	⅝ × 17¹⁵⁄16 × 22³⁄16"	1	Plywood
D	Base	⅝ × 12⁷⁄16 × 17¹⁵⁄16"	1	Plywood
E	Shelf support	⅝ × 8½ × 11⁷⁄16"	2	Plywood
F	Shelf	⅝ × 11⁷⁄16 × 17⅞"	1	Plywood
G	Roof deck	⅝ × 17¼ × 22½"	1	Plywood
H	Front post—left	1½ × 1⅞ × 22¼"	1	Pine
I	Front post—right	1½ × 1⅞ × 19³⁄16"	1	Pine
J	Door header	1½ × 2¾ × 14¾"	1	Pine
K	Doorsill	9⁄16 × 9⁄16 × 14³⁄16"	1	Pine
L	Roof cleat	1½ × 1½ × 18⅜"	1	Pine
M	Eave trim	½ × 1 × 17¼"	1	Pine
N	Corner trim—front/rear	½ × 1½" × cut to fit	4	Pine
O	Corner trim—side	½ × 1" × cut to fit	4	Pine
P	Roofing	17¹⁄16 × 23⅜"	1	26-gauge sheet metal
Q	Roof trim—top	½ × 1½" × cut to fit	3	Pine
R	Roof trim—side	½ × 1" × cut to fit	3	Pine
S	Doorframe—top	¾ × 2³⁄16 × 15½"	1	Pine
T	Doorframe—bottom	¾ × 2³⁄16 × 15¼"	1	Pine
U	Doorframe—left side	¾ × 2³⁄16 × 19⁷⁄16"	1	Pine
V	Doorframe—right side	¾ × 2³⁄16 × 17⁵⁄16"	1	Pine
W	Glazing stop—top	⅜ × ⅜ × 12"	1	Pine
X	Glazing stop—bottom	⅜ × ⅜ × 11¹³⁄16"	1	Pine
Y	Glazing stop—left side	⅜ × ⅜ × 15¾"	1	Pine
Z	Glazing stop—right side	⅜ × ⅜ × 14⅛"	1	Pine
AA	Door glazing	⅛ × 12 × 16"	1	Acrylic glazing

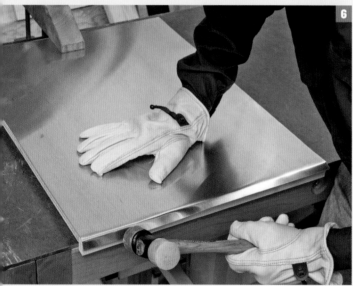

4. Glue the 1″ stock to the face of the 1½″ stock to make 1½″ × 1½″ L-shaped corner trim. 5. Marking the direction of the miter cut on each corner trim helps you orient the piece on your saw when making the final cut to length. 6. Bend the bottom edge of the roofing, using the roof deck, a scrap board, or the edge of your work surface as a bending form. 7. Use the marked lines to fasten the roof deck to the roof cleat and door header.

Apply glue to the side and rear edges of the base and to both side edges of the back panel. Fit the back against the rear edge of the base, then fit the side panels over the edges of the back and base. Make sure all pieces are flush at the bottom and fasten along each edge with three 1⅝-inch trim screws (photo 1).

Add the Shelf Supports

Apply glue to one face of each shelf support, and fit it against a side panel, butted against the base and back panel. Secure each support with four 1-inch screws driven through the support and into the side panel.

The shelf merely rests on top of the shelf supports, so you can remove it as needed to make room for tall items. Put the shelf in a safe place for now and drop it in place later when it's time to fill your structure.

Cut the Front Posts and Door Header

The two front posts and the door header are made from 2 × 4 lumber that is first rip-cut to width before it is cut to length. Each doorpost gets a notch at the bottom to fit over the front edge of the plywood base.

Cut an 8-foot 2 × 4 into two 48-inch pieces, then rip-cut one of the halves to 1⅞ inches wide using a circular saw and a straightedge guide (see Making Straight Cuts on page 31). Using the ripped piece, cut the left and right doorposts to length with a miter saw or miter box, mitering the top ends at 8 degrees and leaving the bottom ends square.

Cut a ⅞-inch-wide × ⁹⁄₁₆-inch-deep notch into the bottom end of each doorpost using a circular saw, jigsaw, or handsaw (photo 2).

Using the remaining half of the 2 × 4, rip-cut a 16-inch section to width at 2¾ inches. Cut the ripped section to length at 14¾ inches, mitering both ends at 8 degrees, so the two miters are parallel. You will use the leftover 2 × 4 lumber later to create the roof cleat.

Install the Front Posts and Header

Apply glue to the right end of the door header. Fit the right doorpost against the glued end so the pieces are perfectly flush at the sides and top. Drill two pilot holes through the outside edge of the post and into the end of the header, then fasten the pieces with two 3-inch screws. Repeat the same process to install the left doorpost at the other end of the header, creating an upside-down U-shaped assembly.

Glue the outside edges of the doorposts and the notches at the bottom ends of the posts. Fit the post-header assembly between the side panels of the box so the notches fit snugly onto the base; they will slide into the spaces created by the doorsill. The top ends and front faces of the posts should be flush with top and front edges of the side panels, respectively.

Fasten the side panels to each post with three 1¾-inch screws (photo 3). Lay the structure on its back. Drill two pilot holes through the base and into each post and fasten the base to the posts with 3-inch screws.

Assemble the Corner and Roof Trim

The four corner trims and three roof trims are L-shaped pieces made by gluing 1-inch-wide stock to 1½-inch-wide stock. It's most efficient to make two long assemblies, then cut all the pieces to length. You will also cut the roof-eave trim from some of the extra 1-inch-wide stock to use later.

Cut one of the 1½-inch and one of the 1-inch pieces of pine stock to length at about 68 inches. Cut the leftover piece of 1-inch stock to length at 17¼ inches and set it aside to use as the roof-eave trim.

Apply glue to one of the side edges of the 68-inch piece of 1-inch stock and fit the piece against the face of the 68-inch piece of 1½-inch stock to form an L shape. Clamp the pieces together in several places. Let the glue dry for at least 1 hour before removing the clamps. Glue together the remaining 8-foot pieces of 1-inch and 1½-inch stock to create another L assembly (photo 4).

Tip: If you don't have enough clamps for the long assembly, you can cut the pieces in 24-inch or 48-inch lengths and glue them up in shorter sections.

Install the Corner Trim

You will use the 8-foot-long trim assembly to cut the four corner trim pieces to length with a miter saw or miter box.

8. Glue the roof-trim angles to the roof deck and tack them in place with finish nails. 9. Fasten each miter joint of the doorframe with a 3" screw driven at a 45° angle.

Plan each cut before making it. Each trim piece is square-cut at the bottom end and miter-cut at the top end at 8 degrees. When installed, the 1-inch-wide piece of each L assembly fits against a side panel so that the joint between the trim boards is visible at the sides of the structure. It's helpful to position each piece on the structure and make a rough reference mark indicating the direction of the miter cut (photo 5).

10. Add the door glazing and reinstall the door after finishing the structure.

Cut the two longer corner trims—for the left side of the structure—to length at 22⁵⁄₁₆ inches. Cut the two shorter corner trims—for the right side of the structure—to length at 19¹¹⁄₁₆ inches. Glue the inside faces of each trim angle, position it on the box so it is flush with the top edges of the plywood panels, and fasten it through the side piece of the angle with three 1¼-inch finish nails.

Prepare the Roof

Glue one face of the roof eave trim and fit it against one of the 17¼-inch edges of the plywood roof deck so the trim is flush with the top face of the deck. Nail the trim in place with three 1¼-inch finish nails.

Cut the sheet metal roofing to size using aviation snips. Bend one of the 17-inch edges at 90 degrees to create a ½-inch wide lip along the bottom edge of the roof (see Working with Sheet Metal on page 37 for tips on working with sheet metal) (photo 6). The lip will fit over the eave trim at the bottom of the roof.

Install the Roof Deck

Cut the roof cleat from a leftover piece of 2 × 4 material: First, rip-cut a 20-inch-long section to 1½ inches wide. Then, cut the ripped piece to length at 18⅜ inches, mitering both ends—with the miters parallel to each other—at 8 degrees.

Glue one face of the roof cleat and position it against the inside face of the back panel, flush with the top edge. Fasten the cleat with three 1⅝-inch trim screws driven through the outside of the back panel.

Draw two lines on the roof deck, parallel to the long edges, for locating the screws that will fasten the roof deck to the roof cleat and the door header. Draw the rear line 3³⁄₁₆ inches from the rear edge of the roof deck; draw the front line 2⁹⁄₁₆ inches from the front edge of the roof deck.

Apply glue to the top edges of the roof cleat and door header. Position the roof deck on the box so it overhangs equally side to side and front to back. Fasten the roof deck to the roof cleat and door header with three 1¾-inch screws each (photo 7).

Complete the Roof

Apply a wavy bead of silicone caulk to the roof deck. Lay the sheet-metal roofing onto the deck so it is centered side to side and the lip at the bottom is snug against the eave trim at the bottom edge of the roof deck. Set a scrap of plywood or scrap boards onto the roofing and clamp the pieces in place. Let the caulk cure overnight, then remove the clamps and scrap wood.

Glue the top edge and side edges of the roof deck. Fit the three roof-trim angles over the top and side edges of the roof so the mitered ends meet snugly at the top corners. Secure each trim piece with three 1-inch finish nails driven through the side of the trim and into the roof deck (photo 8).

Build the Doorframe

Rip-cut an 8-foot-long 1 × 3 board to width at 2³⁄₁₆ inches. Cut a ½ × ½-inch rabbet along at least 72 inches of the board using a circular saw and straightedge guide or a router and ½-inch rabbeting bit (see Making Doors with (or without) Rabbets on page 34 for help with cutting rabbets). You will cut all the doorframe pieces from the rabbeted section of the board.

Note: All of the miter cuts on the doorframe pieces—and the glazing stops—are described as they are viewed from the front of the door. Cut each piece of doorframe to length with the following miters; also cut each corresponding glazing stop to length using the same angles:

Top piece, left end: 49 degrees; top piece, right end: 41 degrees

Left piece, top end: 49 degrees; left piece, bottom end: 45 degrees

Right piece, top end: 41 degrees; right piece, bottom end: 45 degrees

Bottom piece, both ends: 45 degrees

Dry-assemble the doorframe (no glue) and clamp it both directions. Drill a pilot hole at each corner of the frame, angling the hole at 45 degrees through the top/bottom piece and into the side piece. Make sure the hole does not interfere with the rabbet on either piece.

Unclamp the frame pieces, apply glue to the end of each piece, and assemble the frame with a 3-inch wood screw at each joint (photo 9).

Measure the width and height of the doorframe opening, measuring from rabbet to rabbet. Subtract ⅛ inch from each dimension, then cut the door glazing to this size (see Cutting and Drilling Plastic Glazing on page 35). You will install the glazing after painting or staining the project.

Hang the Door

The door is hung with offset-style hinges (sometimes called institutional hinges) that mount to the left doorpost and to the back side of the doorframe. Mount the hinges to the doorframe, about 2½ inches from the top and bottom edges of the frame, using the provided screws.

Position the doorframe so it is aligned with the bottom of the box base and fasten the hinges to the left doorpost with the provided screws. Remove the doorframe and hinges for the finishing process.

Complete the Project

Finish the project as desired (see Painting & Staining on pages 39–42 for finishing tips). When the finish is completely dry, fit the glazing into the rabbets of the doorframe and secure it with the glazing stops, nailed at each end and in the center with 1-inch finish nails. Rehang the door as before (photo 10).

Apply a fine bead of caulk along the edges of the roof trim, to seal the joint where the trim meets the metal roofing. Let the caulk dry overnight.

Position the shelf on top of the shelf supports inside the structure, if desired.

Learn how to register your Little Free Library on page 156.

Tobacco Barn

The Tobacco Barn is a variation on the Cedar Roof Basic (page 97) with some striking decorative differences. Instead of cedar siding for roofing, the Tobacco Barn has tobacco lath—thin wood strips traditionally used for drying tobacco leaves. This unique structure also has tobacco lath decorating the side and rear walls. You can make the lath really pop by painting most of the structure with a neutral solid base color and leaving the lath natural or adding a wood-color stain. You can also leave the doorframe in natural wood tone or paint it with a complementary accent color.

If you look closely at both structures, you'll see that most of the construction is the same, save for the roofing and the wall lath. In fact, to build the Tobacco Barn, you will follow many of the instructions for the Cedar Roof Basic. The steps in which the projects differ are given here.

Now to answer that nagging question: where the heck do you find tobacco lath? You can buy real tobacco lath—that is, salvaged material that was actually used to dry tobacco—from specialty wood suppliers as well as from private salvagers who sell their wares through online marketplaces such as eBay or Etsy. Tobacco lath typically measures 1½ inches wide and ⅜ inch to ½ inch thick, is made of hardwood, and has a rough-cut texture. Fortunately, ordinary wood lath used for traditional plaster walls makes a pretty good substitute, both in size and texture, if not in material. Plaster lath is typically made from construction-grade softwood, such as pine or Douglas fir, but you can stain it to give it the mottled, tobacco-cured look of the real thing. A similar material also is sold in the form of stakes; if you use these, just cut off the pointed ends. Plaster lath and stake slats are commonly sold at lumberyards and home centers.

Author's note: The Tobacco Barn is essentially the Cedar Roof Basic with different roofing and with decorative lath on the side and rear walls. Because most of the steps are identical, I refer the reader to the Cedar Roof Basic for most of the construction, then back here for the final steps (excepting the door, which is the same). Because the lath is irregular and simply butted together, it's not watertight. Therefore, it's best to finish

1. The gable trim covers the ends of the eave trim and is flush with the surface of the roof deck. 2. Install the roof cap with construction adhesive and 1½" finish nails.

the box, roof deck, and lath before adding the lath as the final step (before rehanging the door).

Construction differences with the Tobacco Barn:

Gable trim is shorter and is flush with surface of roof deck. Roof cap sits directly on roof deck and is fastened with shorter nails.

All wood parts (including lath) are finished before lath goes on.

Final note: In the original Little Free Library project, the builders ripped the roof slats to 1¼ inches wide, probably for looks but perhaps to make the butt joints a bit tighter. In any case, it's not worth doing this unless you have a tablesaw, so I specified full lath slats for the roof. This creates a ½-inch overhang at the eaves.

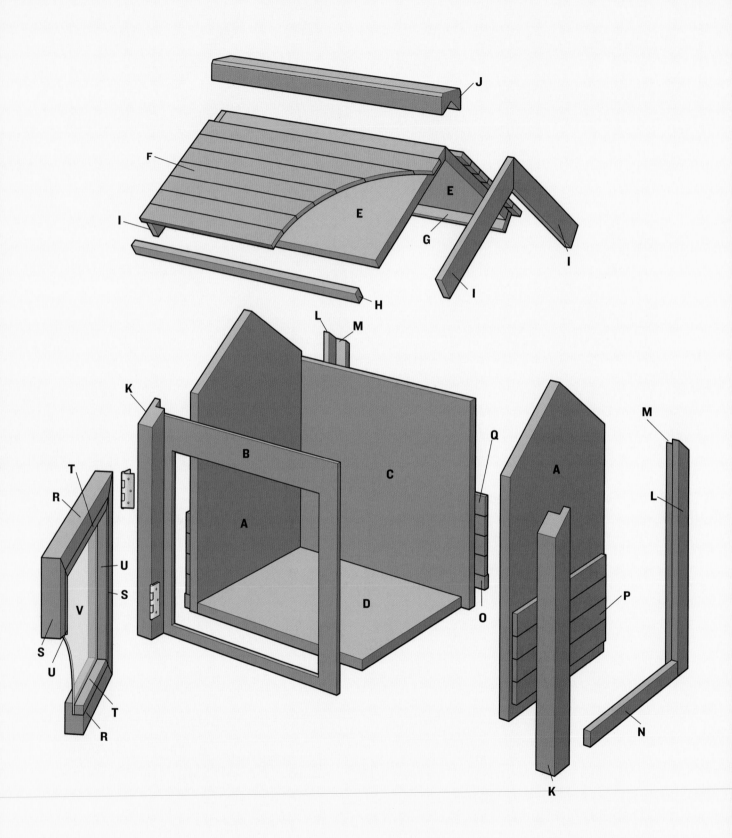

TOOLS & MATERIALS

Circular saw
Jigsaw
Router and ¾" rabbeting
  bit (optional)
Clamps
Straightedge
Drill-driver
Drill bits (¹⁄₁₆", ⅜")
Pilot-countersink bit
Screwdriver bits
Miter saw or miter box
Hammer

Nail set
Caulking gun
Sanding block
4 × 8' sheet of ¾" plywood
2 × 2' piece of ¼" plywood
½ × 1½ × 96" pine
½ × 1¾ × 48" pine
(2) 2 × 3" (nominal) × 6' pine
½ × 1 × 96" pine
⅝ × ⅝ × 48" pine
(11) ⅜ × 1½ × 48" tobacco lath
(35) 1¾" wood screws

(6) 2½" finish nails
(4) 1½" finish nails
(51) 1¼" finish nails
(72) 1" siding nails
⅛ × 12 × 16" acrylic glazing
(2) exterior door hinges with screws
Waterproof wood glue
Construction adhesive
100-grit sandpaper
Eye and ear protection
Work gloves

CUTTING LIST

KEY	PART	DIMENSIONS	PCS.	MATERIAL
A	Side panel	¾ × 13 × 20¾"	2	¾" plywood
B	Front panel	¼ × 17⅛ × 15¾"	1	¼" plywood
C	Back panel	¾ × 17⅛ × 15½"	1	¾" plywood
D	Base	¾ × 15¹¹⁄₁₆ × 13"	1	¾" plywood
E	Roof deck	¾ × 21 × 10¾"	2	¾" plywood
F	Roofing	⅜ × 1½ × 22¼"	14	Tobacco lath
G	Roof eave trim—rear	½ × 1½ × 21"	1	Pine
H	Roof eave trim—front	½ × ⅞ × 21"	1	Pine
I	Roof-gable trim	½ × 1¾ × 11½"	4	Pine
J	Roof cap	1½ × 2½ × 22"	1	Pine
K	Front-corner trim	1⅜ × 1⅞ × 16⁵⁄₁₆"	2	Pine
L	Rear-corner trim—side	½ × 1½ × 16¼"	2	Pine
M	Rear-corner trim—rear	½ × 1 × 15⅝"	2	Pine
N	Base trim—side	½ × 1 × 12½"	2	Pine
O	Base trim—rear	½ × 1 × 15¹⁄₁₆"	1	Pine
P	Sidewall lath	⅜ × 1½ × 12⁹⁄₁₆"	8	Tobacco lath
Q	Rear wall lath	⅜ × 1½ × 15⅛"	4	Tobacco lath
R	Doorframe—top/bottom	1¼ × 2 × 15"	2	Pine
S	Doorframe—side	1¼ × 2 × 14"	2	Pine
T	Glazing stop—top/bottom	⅝ × ⅝ × 12¼"	2	Pine
U	Glazing stop—side	⅝ × ⅝ × 11³⁄₁₆"	2	Pine
V	Door glazing	⅛ × 12 × 16"	1	Acrylic glazing

3. Fit the roofing slats tightly together and secure them with siding nails, three per slat. The roof deck and the slats have been finished with paint and clearcoat, respectively. 4. Install the wall lath from the bottom up, fitting it between the corner trims on the box.

INSTRUCTIONS

Complete the Box Construction

Complete the basic box construction following the instructions on pages 97–102, stopping at the end of the procedure for "Prepare the Roof Deck."

Here's how this works: The project steps for the Cedar Roof Basic and the Tobacco Barn are identical until you get to the roofing. Also, the door construction is the same for both projects. The main difference with the Tobacco Barn is that you will finish all the wood parts before you install the roofing and wall lath. All of the lath goes on at the end and is purely for decoration. It's important that you finish all of the parts before installing the lath because

the layer created by the lath isn't reliably watertight. The finish underneath the lath will protect the wood if moisture gets between the lath strips.

Add the Roof Gable Trim

Cut the four pieces of roof gable trim to length at 11½ inches, mitering the top ends at 36 degrees. Apply glue to the side edges of the roof deck panels and outside ends of the roof eave trim. Also glue the mitered edges of the gable trim.

Position the gable trim pieces in pairs at each end of the roof, joining each pair of miters together at the peak. The top of the trim should be flush with the top faces of the roof deck panels. The bottom ends of the trim should be flush with the exposed faces of the eave trim (photo 1). Fasten each piece of gable trim to the roof deck with three 1¼-inch finish nails.

Cut and Install the Roof Cap

Follow the instructions on page 102 to cut the V-groove in the roof cap, cut the cap to length, and sand its edges. To install the roof cap, apply a bead of construction adhesive to each side of the V-groove. Position the cap at the roof peak so it is flush with the outside faces of the roof-gable trim at both ends. Drill ⅛-inch pilot holes—through the cap only—and nail the cap to the roof with four 1½-inch finish nails (photo 2).

Build and Hang the Door

Follow the instructions on page 103 to build the doorframe and prepare the glazing and glazing stops. Hang the doorframe on the structure with hinges, then remove the frame and hinges for the finishing process. You will install the door glazing and stops and rehang the door after finishing.

Finish the Wood

Apply a finish to the entire exterior of the structure (see Painting & Staining on pages 39–42 for finishing tips). Also finish the interior, if desired. Cut the roofing and side and rear wall lath pieces to length. Finish all surfaces of the lath with an exterior stain or clear coat finish. Allow all finishes to dry completely.

Install the Roofing

Drill three ⅛-inch pilot holes in each roofing slat, making one hole about 1½ inches from each end and one hole at the center.

Install the roofing lath from the top down: Apply a bead of construction adhesive to the back side of one of the roofing slats. Place the slat on the roof deck so it is butted against the roof cap and overhangs the gable trim equally on both sides of the roof. Fasten the slat with three 1-inch siding nails driven through the pilot holes (you can also use 1-inch coated ring-shank paneling nails, which are smaller and less visible than siding nails).

Install the remaining roofing slats to complete the roof side, butting the slats tightly together as you go (photo 3). The bottom slat will overhang the eave trim by about ½ inch, depending on the width of the slats. Install the slats on the other side of the roof.

Install the Wall Slats and Door

Drill two ¹⁄₁₆-inch pilot holes in each side- and rear-wall lath slat, making one hole about 1½ inches from each end.

Install four sidewall slats on each side of the structure using construction adhesive and 1-inch siding nails (or paneling nails) driven through the pilot holes. Start at the bottom of each wall, fitting the slat between the front- and rear-corner trims and butting it against the base trim. Fit the pieces tightly together before nailing each piece (photo 4).

Install the four rear-wall lath slats, using the same techniques and fitting the slats between the rear-corner trims.

Complete the door by fitting the glazing into the rabbets of the doorframe and securing it with the glazing stops, nailed at each end and in the center with 1¼-inch finish nails. Rehang the door as before.

Learn how to register your Little Free Library on page 156.

Cedar Roof Basic

This tiny structure is named for its attractive roof made from rough cedar siding. It's also one of the few designs with a gable roof and a door under the roof eave rather than on the gable end. This gives it a distinctive look and makes it easier to access the interior space.

The roofing material is beveled siding, also called lap siding or clapboard. It is tapered so the bottom edge is thicker than the top edge. Each piece overlaps the piece below to create a stepped shingle effect. Traditional cedar siding has a smooth side and a rough side. The rough side usually faces out and looks best when finished with a stain or even a clear coat (see Painting & Staining on page 39) to retain the natural grain and coloring. If you prefer to paint the roof, you might install the boards with the smooth side up for a cleaner look.

Another option for this project is to use salvaged siding or lumber for the roofing or any of the trim details. Since the main structure is a basic and easy-to-build plywood box, it's up to the roofing and trim to provide extra character. Don't be afraid to get creative!

INSTRUCTIONS

Cut the Plywood Parts

Cut the side panels, front panel, back panel, base, and roof deck pieces to size using a circular saw or jigsaw. All pieces are rectangular except for the side panels, which have triangular top ends. The roof deck pieces get a bevel along one long edge after the pieces are cut to size.

To lay out the triangular cuts on each side panel, mark the center of one of the short sides, then make a mark 4⅝ inches down each side edge. Draw a line from each side mark to the center mark. Cut along the lines.

To make the bevel cuts on the roof deck pieces, set up a straightedge guide (see Making Straight Cuts on page 31) to cut ⁵⁄₁₆ inch from one of the long edges. Set a circular saw or jigsaw to cut a 36-degree bevel, and make the cut (photo 1). A tablesaw is even better, if you have one.

Cut the Door Opening

The front panel gets a rectangular cutout for the door opening that is 13⅞ inches wide × 12⅝ inches tall. Mark this rectangle on the front panel so it is centered side to side and the bottom of the rectangle is 1¹⁄₁₆ inches from the

1. The bevel on the roof deck will span about half the thickness of the plywood. 2. Drill a starter hole at each corner, then make the door cutout with a jigsaw. Be sure to cut the narrow sides first. 3. The front and back panels fit over the sides, and all vertical pieces fit over the base.

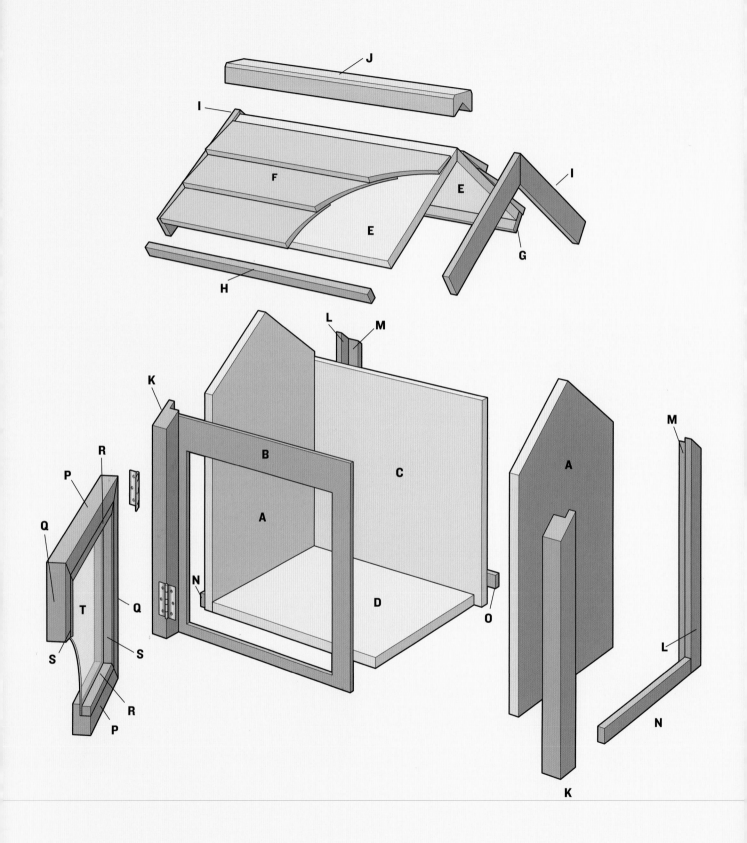

TOOLS & MATERIALS

Circular saw
Jigsaw
Router and ¾" rabbeting bit
 (optional)
Clamps
Straightedge
Drill-driver
Drill bits (¹⁄₁₆", ³⁄₈")
Pilot-countersink bit
Screwdriver bits
Miter saw or miter box
Hammer

Nail set
Caulking gun
Sanding block
4 × 8' sheet of ¾" plywood
2 × 2' piece of ¼" plywood
⅝ × 5⅛ × 96" beveled cedar siding
1 ⅝ × 5⅛ × 48" beveled cedar siding
½ × 1½ × 96" pine
½ × 1¾ × 48" pine
(2) 2 × 3 (nominal) × 6' pine
½ × 1 × 96" pine
⅝ × ⅝ × 48" pine

(23) 1¾" wood screws
(12) 1" wood screws
(10) 2½" finish nails
(51) 1¼" finish nails
(36) 1" siding nails
⅛ × 12 × 16" acrylic glazing
(2) exterior door hinges with screws
Waterproof wood glue
Construction adhesive
100-grit sandpaper
Eye and ear protection
Work gloves

CUTTING LIST

KEY	PART	DIMENSIONS	PCS.	MATERIAL
A	Side panel	¾ × 13 × 20¾"	2	¾" plywood
B	Front panel	¼ × 17⅛ × 15¹¹⁄₁₆"	1	¼" plywood
C	Back panel	¾ × 17⅛ × 15⁷⁄₁₆"	1	¾" plywood
D	Base	¾ × 15¹¹⁄₁₆ × 13"	1	¾" plywood
E	Roof deck	¾ × 21 × 10¾"	2	¾" plywood
F	Roofing	⅝ × 5⅛ × 21"	6	Cedar siding
G	Roof eave trim—rear	½ × 1½ × 21"	1	Pine
H	Roof eave trim—front	½ × ⅞ × 21"	1	Pine
I	Roof-gable trim	½ × 1¾ × 11¾"	4	Pine
J	Roof cap	1½ × 2½ × 22"	1	Pine
K	Front-corner trim	1⅜ × 1⅞ × 16⁵⁄₁₆"	2	Pine
L	Rear-corner trim—side	½ × 1½ × 16¼"	2	Pine
M	Rear-corner trim—rear	½ × 1 × 15⅝"	2	Pine
N	Base trim—side	½ × 1 × 12½"	2	Pine
O	Base trim—rear	½ × 1 × 15¹⁄₁₆"	1	Pine
P	Doorframe—top/bottom	1¼ × 2 × 15"	2	Pine
Q	Doorframe—side	1¼ × 2 × 14"	2	Pine
R	Glazing stop—top/bottom	⅝ × ⅝ × 12¼"	2	Pine
S	Glazing stop—side	⅝ × ⅝ × 11³⁄₁₆"	2	Pine
T	Door glazing	⅛ × 12 × 16"	1	Acrylic glazing

4. The ½"-wide rabbet is cut ⅞" deep into 1⅞" face of the trim material. 5. The rear-corner side pieces fit over the edges of the rear-corner rear pieces. 6. The roof deck panels meet at the roof peak and overhang the box sides equally. 7. Fasten the roofing boards so the lower nails go through the roofing board below.

bottom edge of the panel. Drill a ⅜-inch starter hole (see Making Curves and Interior Cutouts on page 32) on the inside of each corner of the rectangle, then make the cutout with a jigsaw (photo 2).

Assemble the Box

Apply wood glue to both side edges and the rear edge of the plywood base and to the rear-side edge of each side panel. Assemble the base, sides, and back so the base fits inside the assembly and the back panel fits over the edges of the side panels. Clamp the parts together. Fasten the pieces with three 1¾-inch screws along each joint.

Glue the front edges of the base and side panels. Fit the front panel over the sides and base so all pieces are flush on the outside and the bottom. Fasten through the front panel and into the sides and base with three 1-inch screws along each edge (photo 3).

Prepare the Front-Corner Trim

The two front-corner trim pieces are first rip-cut from 2 × 3 lumber. Then they each get a ½ × ⅞-inch rabbet cut along one long edge, creating a lip that overlaps the corner of the plywood box (see Making Doors with [or without] Rabbets on page 34 for help with cutting rabbets). They are also mitered on their top ends at 36 degrees. It's easiest to make the long rip cuts and rabbet on a single piece of 2 × 3, then cut the trim to final size with a miter saw or miter box.

Cut a 6-foot 2 × 3 roughly in half and set one of the halves aside; you will use it later for the roof cap. Use a straightedge guide to rip-cut the 2 × 3 to 1⅞ inches wide × 1⅜ inches thick. Then, cut a ½-inch-wide × ⅞-inch-deep rabbet using a router and ½-inch rabbeting bit or a circular saw and straightedge guide (photo 4). Cut each trim piece to length, mitering the top end at 36 degrees.

Install the Front-Corner Trim

Apply glue to both sides of the rabbet on each piece of front-corner trim. Position the trim at the front corner of the box assembly so the top (mitered) end of the trim is flush with the angled top edge of the side panel and the lip is up against the side panel. Drill ¹⁄₁₆-inch pilot holes, and fasten each trim piece with three 2½-inch finish nails driven through the front of the trim and into the edges of the side panels. Set the nails with a nail set.

Install the Remaining Box Trim

Cut the rear-corner trim side and rear pieces to length, mitering their top ends at 36 degrees. The side pieces are mitered across their 1½-inch faces. The rear pieces are mitered across their ½-inch edges. Apply glue to the longer 1-inch-wide face of each rear piece and position it over the back panel, flush with the outside edge and bottom of the panel. Fasten each trim piece with three 1¼-inch finish nails.

Apply glue to the inside face of each side trim piece and position it over a rear trim piece so their mitered ends are flush. Fasten the side trim to the box with three 1¼-inch finish nails (photo 5).

Cut the base trim side and rear pieces to length. Apply glue to one face of the rear trim and fit it against the back, between the rear-corner trims and flush with the bottom of the base. Fasten the rear trim with three 1¼-inch finish nails. Do the same with the two base trim side pieces, fitting them between the front- and rear-corner trims.

Prepare the Roof Deck

Cut the two roof eave trim pieces to length. Glue the front (⅞-inch-wide) trim to the bottom (square) edge of one of the roof panels so it is flush with the top face and side edges of the panel; it will overhang the bottom face of the panel by about ⅛ inch. Fasten the trim with three 1¼-inch finish nails.

Glue and nail the rear (1½-inch-wide) eave trim to the other roof deck panel so the trim is flush with the top face and side edges of the panel, overhanging the bottom face.

Apply glue to the top edges of the side panels. Fit the roof deck panels onto the side panels so they meet at

8. The gable trim covers the ends of the eave trim, the roof deck, and the overlapping portions of the roofing boards. **9.** Make opposing 1½"-deep bevel cuts to create the V-groove in the roof cap. **10.** Drill pilot holes at a 45° angle for joining the mitered doorframe pieces with screws.

11. Add the door glazing and reinstall the door after finishing the structure.

the roof peak and overhang the side panels equally on both sides (photo 6). Fasten each roof deck panel to the side panels with four 1¾-inch screws.

Install the Roofing

Cut the six roofing boards to length. Rip-cut two of the boards to width at 4⅜ inches, ripping about ¾ inch from the top (narrow) edge of the beveled siding board. The ripped boards will go at the top of the roof.

Apply a wavy bead of construction adhesive to the back side (smooth face) of one of the full-width boards. Position it at the bottom of one of the roof deck pieces so the roofing overhangs the bottom face of the eave trim by about ⅛ inch. Nail the roofing board to the roof deck with three pairs of 1-inch siding nails, with one pair about 1 inch from each end and one pair in the center. If the nails cause the wood to split, drill pilot holes for the nails.

Apply a straight bead of construction adhesive near the top and bottom edges of a second roofing board. Place the board on the roof deck so it overlaps the first board by about 1¾ inches (leaving about 3⅜ inches of the lower board

exposed). Nail the second board with three pairs of nails, as with the first board, but make sure the lower nail in each pair goes through the first board.

Apply adhesive near the top and bottom edges of one of the ripped boards, position it so it is flush with the top edge of the roof deck, and nail it as with the second board (photo 7). Repeat the same process to install the roofing boards on the other side of the roof.

Add the Roof Gable Trim

Cut the four pieces of roof gable trim to length, mitering the top ends at 36 degrees. Apply glue to the side edges of the roof deck panels and outside ends of the roof eave trim. Also glue the mitered edges of the gable trim.

Position the gable trim in pairs at each end of the roof, joining the miters together at the peak. The gable trim at the rear eave of the roof should be flush with the bottom edge and front face of the 1½-inch-wide eave trim. At the front eave of the roof, the gable trim will overhang the top and bottom edge of the ⅞-inch-wide eave trim (photo 8).

Fasten each piece of gable trim to the roof deck (not the roofing boards) with three 1¼-inch finish nails.

Cut and Install the Roof Cap

The roof cap is cut from the remaining piece of 2 × 3 board (leftover from the front corner trim). It has a V-shaped groove cut into its bottom face that runs along the entire length of the board. You can cut the groove with a small circular saw and a straightedge guide (or use a tablesaw, if you have one). This is a tricky cut and is not recommended for beginners to try with a full-size circular saw. As an alternative, you can make 36-degree bevel cuts on two ¾-inch-thick boards and use waterproof wood glue to join them to create the V shape.

Set the circular saw blade to make a 36-degree bevel cut, 1½ inches deep. Position the 2 × 3 on one of its 1½-inch-wide edges, and set up a straightedge guide with a scrap board to support the saw (see Making Straight Cuts on page 31). Make the first cut from the corner of the 2 × 3 to its center. Rotate the board end-for-end and make the second cut to meet the first cut at the center of the board's thickness (photo 9).

Cut the roof cap to length. Sand the four corners of the board to create a slight chamfer (beveled edge) for a finished look using sandpaper and a sanding block. (You can also use a tablesaw to cut the corner chamfers.) Apply a bead of construction adhesive to both sides of the V-groove. Position the cap at the roof peak so it is flush with the outside faces of the roof gable trim at both ends. Drill ¹⁄₁₆-inch pilot holes and nail the cap to the roof with four 2½-inch finish nails, angling the nails so they don't poke through the interior side of the roof deck.

Build and Hang the Door

Rip-cut a 6-foot 2 × 3 board to size at 1¼ inches thick × 2 inches wide using a circular saw and a straightedge guide (or use a tablesaw). Cut a ¾ × ¾-inch rabbet along one edge of the ripped board using a circular saw or a router and ¾-inch rabbeting bit. Using the prepared board, cut the doorframe sides and top and bottom to length, mitering their ends at 45 degrees.

Dry-assemble (no glue) the doorframe and clamp it both directions. Drill two countersunk pilot holes at each corner of the frame, angling the holes through the top/bottom piece and into each side piece (photo 10). Make sure the holes do not interfere with the rabbet on either piece.

Note: If you don't want to rabbet the doorframe pieces, you can cut the glazing a little larger and mount it to the back side of the assembled frame (see Making Doors with [or without] Rabbets on page 34).

Unclamp the frame pieces, apply glue to the ends of each piece, and assemble the frame with two 1¾-inch wood screws at each joint.

Cut the glazing stops from ⅝ × ⅝-inch stock, mitering both ends at 45 degrees. Measure the width and height of the doorframe opening, measuring from rabbet to rabbet. Subtract ⅛ inch from each dimension, then cut the door glazing to this size (see Cutting and Drilling Plastic Glazing on page 35). You will install the glazing after finishing the project.

Mount the door hinges to the doorframe using the provided screws. You can hang the door from either side of the structure, depending on which way you want the door to swing. Mount the door to either of the front corner trim pieces, aligning the bottom of the doorframe with the bottom ends of the front corner trim.

Complete the Project

Remove the door and hinges. Finish the project as desired (see Painting & Staining on pages 39–42 for finishing tips). When the finish is completely dry, fit the glazing into the rabbets of the doorframe and secure it with the glazing stops, nailed at each end and in the center with a 1¼-inch finish nail. Rehang the door as before (photo 11).

Learn how to register your Little Free Library on page 156.

First Little Free Library

The idea that spawned tens of thousands of free book exchanges around the world started with one tiny schoolhouse library in Hudson, Wisconsin. It was built by Todd Bol, in honor of his mother, a former schoolteacher and lifelong reader. Bol built his library partially out of an old 1920s garage door salvaged from his own house. He mounted the tiny structure in his front yard and filled it with books, and the idea grew.

This little structure is a replica of Bol's very first library and includes many of its charming details, from the stepped roofing to the prominent trim boards to the tiny windows made from little pieces of wood molding. The side and back walls are made with special grooved plywood to resemble traditional siding. The distinctive façade includes a horizontal ledge board over the door, a deep roof eave, and decorative trim boards that span across the roof planes.

The custom detailing of this project makes it a little more complicated to build than most of the other designs in this book, but the results are worth the effort. A power miter saw, or even a manual miter box, will make the numerous angle cuts much easier. As for materials, you can follow the instructions to the letter, or take a cue from the original builder and work in some salvaged items you've been saving for something special.

INSTRUCTIONS

Cut the Plywood Parts

Cut the side panels, front gable, back panel, and roof deck pieces using a circular saw or jigsaw and following the dimensions in the cutting list (page 107) and the diagram on page 106.

Bevel the top edges of the side panels and the roof deck pieces at 26 degrees (photo 1). This is the same angle you will use for all of the cuts that follow the roof slope.

To mark the triangular tops of the back panel and front gable, first mark the center along the top edge of the piece. On each side of the front gable, measure down 4$\frac{5}{16}$ inches and make a mark. Draw a straight line between each side mark and the center mark. Do the same with the back gable, measuring down 4$\frac{5}{8}$ inches on the sides.

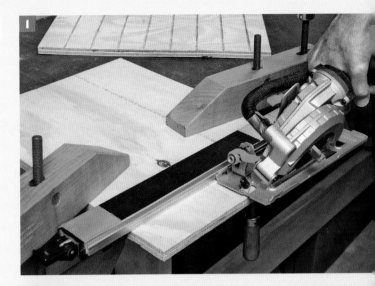

1. Set your circular saw or jigsaw to cut a 26° angle for the side and roof pieces. 2. Assemble the front frame with glue and 3" screws. 3. The roof cleats on the back panel should be $\frac{5}{8}$" from the back panel's side edges.

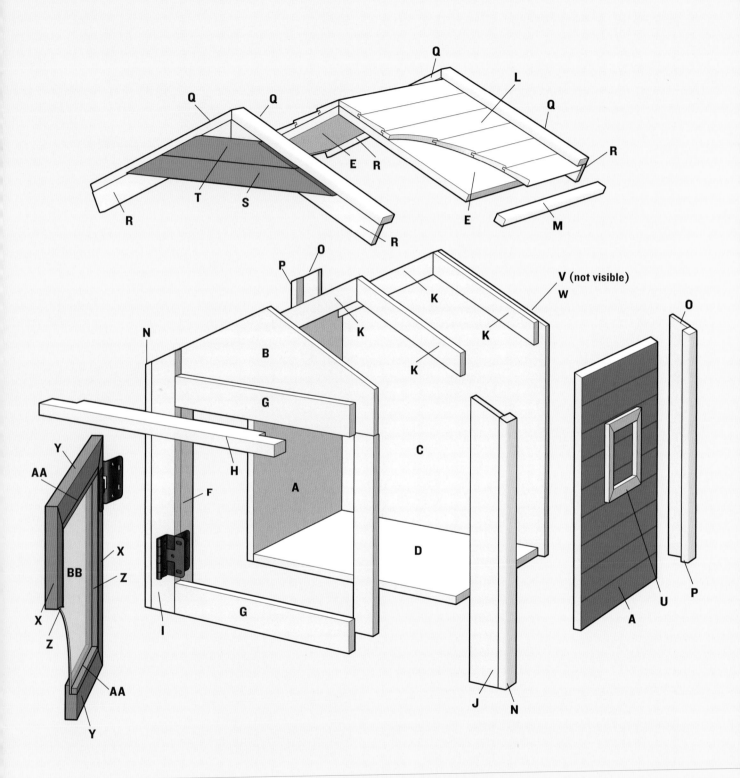

TOOLS & MATERIALS

Circular saw or jigsaw
Clamps
Drill-driver
Pilot-countersink bit
Screwdriver bits (as needed for screws)
Miter saw or miter box
48 × 48" piece of ⅝" grooved plywood
24 × 48" piece of ⅝" plywood
(2) 1 × 3 (nominal) × 8' pine
2 × 2 (nominal) × 13¾" pine

1 × 2 (nominal) × 6' pine
(3) ½ × 2½" × 8' pine tongue-and-groove siding
(4) 9/16 × 1½" × 8' pine mullion molding
⅜ × ¾" × 8' pine
⅜ × ⅜ × 48" pine
(24) 1⅝" trim screws
(17) 1½" wood screws
(3) 1¾" wood screws
(12) 3" wood screws

(25) 1¼" wood screws
(64) 1" finish nails
(40) ⅞" finish nails
Waterproof wood glue
Paintable exterior caulk
Wood finishing supplies (as needed)
⅛ × 18 × 24" acrylic glazing
(2) exterior offset hinges (for ¾" doorframe) with screws
Eye and ear protection
Work gloves

CUTTING LIST

KEY	PART	DIMENSIONS	PCS.	MATERIAL
A	Side panel	⅝ × 13 × 17⅝"	2	⅝" grooved plywood
B	Front gable	⅝ × 18 1/16 × 7½"	1	⅝" plywood
C	Back panel	⅝ × 19¼ × 22"	1	⅝" grooved plywood
D	Base	⅝ × 13 × 18 1/16"	1	⅝" plywood
E	Roof deck	⅝ × 12⅜ × 16½"	2	⅝" plywood
F	Front frame—side	¾ × 2⅛ × 18⅜"	2	Pine
G	Front frame—top/bottom	¾ × 2⅛ × 15"	2	Pine
H	Front frame—top ledge board	¾ × 2⅛ × 19 3/16"	1	Pine
I	Front frame—hinge cleat	1½ × 1½ × 13¾"	1	Pine
J	Front frame—latch cleat	¾ × 1½ × 13¼"	1	Pine
K	Roof cleat	¾ × 1¼ × 10 7/16"	4	Pine
L	Roofing plank	½ × 2½ × 16½"	12	Pine siding
M	Roof eave trim	9/16 × ¾ × 16½"	2	Pine molding
N	Front-side trim	9/16 × 1½ × 17¼"	2	Pine molding
O	Rear-corner trim—back	9/16 × 1½ × 18"	2	Pine molding
P	Rear-corner trim—side	9/16 × 1½" × cut to fit	2	Pine molding
Q	Roof trim—top	9/16 × 1½ × 13½"	4	Pine molding
R	Roof trim—side	9/16 × 1½" × cut to fit	4	Pine molding
S	Front-gable trim—lower	9/16 × 1½ × 17 1/16"	1	Pine molding
T	Front-gable trim—upper	9/16 × 1½ × 11 5/16"	1	Pine molding
U	Window frame	⅜ × ¾ × 5½"	10	Pine
V	Window frame—long	⅜ × ¾ × 9⅛"	2	Pine
W	Window mullion	⅜ × ¾ × 4"	1	Pine
X	Doorframe—side	¾ × 2⅛ × 13 5/16"	2	Pine
Y	Doorframe—top/bottom	¾ × 2⅛ × 16"	2	Pine
Z	Glazing stop—side	⅜ × ⅜ × 9¾"	2	Pine
AA	Glazing stop—top/bottom	⅜ × ⅜ × 12½"	2	Pine
BB	Door glazing	⅛ × 18 × 24"	1	Acrylic glazing

Prepare the Front Frame Pieces

Rip-cut two 8-foot 1 × 3 boards to a width of 2⅛ inches. Use one of these pieces to cut the front frame sides, top and bottom, and top ledge board to length. The side pieces are mitered at 26 degrees. You will use the remaining ripped board later for the doorframe.

Cut a 2⅛-inch-wide × ¾-inch-deep notch at each end of the top ledge board. These notches will accept the side pieces in the assembly. Cut the hinge cleat to length from 2 × 2 lumber, and cut the latch cleat to length from 1 × 2 lumber.

Apply glue to the top edge of the front frame top piece. Position the top ledge on the glued edge so the ends of the frame top are flush with the notches on the ledge board and both pieces are flush at the back. Clamp the pieces together and let the glue dry for at least 1 hour before removing the clamps.

Assemble the Front Frame

Apply glue to the ends of the front frame top and bottom boards. Place the front frame top (with the top ledge board attached) and the front frame bottom between the two front frame side pieces. The bottom piece should be flush with the square ends of the sides. The top ledge should be flush with the shorter edge of the angled tops of the sides. Clamp the assembly, drill pilot holes (see Screwing and Nailing in Wood on page 33), and fasten through the sides and into the ends of the bottom and top frame pieces with two 3-inch screws at each joint (photo 2).

Determine which way the door should open; the hinges can go on either side of the front frame. Apply glue and position the hinge cleat on the back side of the front frame so its top end is aligned with the bottom edge of the front frame top piece and its long edge is flush with the inside edge of the side piece. Fasten the hinge cleat with three 1¾-inch screws. Install the latch cleat in the same position on the other side of the frame opening using three 1¼-inch screws.

4. Driving trim screws through the front frame side pieces and into side panels, assemble the box so all angled pieces are flush at the top. **5.** Assemble the Ls so there is a ¹⁄₁₆" lip (called a "reveal") along the overlapped piece. **6.** The roof deck overhangs the back of the box by ½" and the front by about 2¾". **7.** The back sides of the roof planks lie flat against the roof deck; the front sides are stepped like clapboard siding. **8.** The front-gable trim installs over the front faces of the roof-trim Ls. **9.** The mullion trim fits between the long window pieces to create the effect of a double window.

Add the Roof Cleats

Cut the four roof cleats to length from 1 × 2 lumber. Each piece is mitered at 26 degrees on both ends, with the miters facing the same direction. Install the roof cleats in pairs to the inside faces of the back panel and the front gable; the cleats meet at the point and should be flush with the top edges of the plywood pieces (photo 3). Secure each cleat with glue and two 1¼-inch screws.

Assemble the Box

Apply glue to the rear edge of each side panel. Fit the side panels against the back panel so all top edges are flush. Fasten through the back panel and into each side panel with three 1⅝-inch trim screws.

Glue all four edges of the base piece. Position it between the sides and back so all pieces are flush on the bottom. Glue the front edges of both side panels. Fit the front frame against the edges of the sides. Fasten the front frame to the sides, the sides to the base, and the back panel to the base with three 1⅝-inch trim screws at each joint (photo 4). **Note:** Trim screws have small heads, so you don't need countersunk pilot holes—just straight pilot holes.

Apply glue to the interior side of the top ledge board and the front frame top piece. Fit the front gable between the side panels and up against the front frame so all the angles are flush at the top. Drive three 1¼-inch screws through the inside of the front gable and into the front frame top piece.

Prepare the Trim

All trim pieces are cut from 1½-inch-wide mullion molding, which is flat trim with slightly rounded edges on the top face. The rounded edges always face out. The rear-corner trims and roof trims are L-shaped and are each made with two pieces of molding glued and nailed to form a right angle. It's easiest to cut the pieces a little long and assemble them into Ls before mitering the top ends to the finished length.

Cut the rear-corner trim pieces a little longer than specified in the cutting list. Assemble them in pairs using glue and four 1-inch finish nails to form the two Ls. The trick here is not to overlap the pieces completely; offset the overlap by about 1/16 inch so that the rounded edge is exposed at the outside of the corner (photo 5). Cut each L to the final length, mitering one end at 26 degrees using a miter saw or miter box. Repeat the same process to create the four roof trim assemblies.

Cut the two front-side trim pieces to length, mitering the ends at 26 degrees. Cut the front-gable trim pieces with long 26-degree miters at each end. Finally, rip-cut a piece of mullion molding to a width of ⅞ inch, then cut it into two pieces at 16½ inches each; these are the roof eave trim pieces.

Install the Box Trim

Install the rear-corner trims over the back corner of the box so the top edges of the trim are flush with the angled edges of the side and back panels. Secure the trim with glue and 1-inch finish nails. Install the front-side trim with glue and

Add the Roofing Planks

The roof planks are 2½-inch-wide tongue-and-groove siding boards that are glued and nailed to the plywood roof deck panels. Cut 12 planks to length at 16½ inches. You will install the planks from the top down, starting with two beveled pieces at the top.

Rip-cut the two top pieces to 2⅛ inches wide, beveling the top edges at 26 degrees. Apply glue to the back side of each piece, then apply a bead of exterior caulk along the beveled edge of one of the planks. Fit the pieces onto the roof so they meet at the roof peak. Secure each plank with a ⅞-inch finish nail near each end. Nail close enough to the ends so the nail holes will be covered by the trim.

Install four more planks on each side of the roof using glue and nails and fitting the tongue-and-groove joints together. For the sixth plank on each side, trim off about ¼ inch to ⅜ inch from the grooved edge of the plank, leaving a solid (no groove) edge that overhangs the roof eave trim by about ⅛ inch (photo 7). Install the last pieces with glue and nails.

Complete the Roof Trim

The roof is trimmed with the four L-shaped roof-trim assemblies and the two front-gable trim pieces. To install the Ls, apply glue to the front and rear edges of the roof deck and the ends of the roofing planks. Fit the Ls together in pairs so they meet at the roof peak. Nail the Ls to the roof with 1-inch finish nails.

Position the lower (longer) front-gable trim piece over the front of both Ls at the front of the roof. Align the mitered edges of the gable trim with the vertical pieces of the Ls and fasten the gable trim with 1-inch finish nails. The nails should go into the roof deck and not stick out below the deck. Install the upper (shorter) gable trim above the lower gable trim so the pieces are touching (photo 8).

Create the Windows

The box gets a square window on each side and a rectangular window at the back. Cut the window frame pieces from ⅜ × ¾-inch pine stock, mitering them at 45 degrees so they fit together like a picture frame.

Draw a horizontal line at the center of each sidewall, 8¼ inches up from the bottom of the side panel. Apply glue to the back side of one of the 5½-inch window-frame pieces. Position the trim so its bottom edge is on the pencil line and it is centered side to side on the side panel. Nail the trim near each end with a 1-inch finish nail.

10. Drill pilot holes for screws that will go through the top/bottom piece and into each side piece at an angle. **11.** Offset hinges have right-angle bends that fit together when the door is closed.

nails so the trim covers the outside edge of each front frame side and the pieces are flush at the front.

Install the Roof Deck

Install a piece of roof eave trim to the bottom (square, not angled) edge of each roof deck panel using glue and 1-inch finish nails. The square edge of the eave trim should be flush with the top face of the roof deck and the ends flush as the sides of the roof deck.

Glue the top faces of the roof cleats and the top plywood edges of the box. Set one of the roof deck pieces onto the box so it overhangs the back panel by about ½ inch (photo 6). Set the other roof deck in place so the two pieces meet at the peak of the roof. Fasten each roof deck piece to each cleat with two 1¼-inch screws.

Apply glue to three more 5½-inch trim pieces and fit them together around the installed piece to create a four-sided window frame. Nail the pieces with finish nails. Repeat the same process to create a window frame on the other sidewall.

Mark the back wall at 8¼ inches and install the long window frame using two 9⅛-inch pieces for the top and bottom and two 5½-inch pieces for the sides. Finally, install the window mullion centered in the long window frame (photo 9).

Build the Doorframe

Using the remaining 8-foot 1 × 3 board (which you ripped to 2⅛-inch wide), cut a ½ × ½-inch rabbet along at least 60 inches of the board (see Making Doors with (or without) Rabbets on page 34 for help with cutting rabbets). Using the rabbeted section of the board, cut the doorframe sides and top and bottom, mitering their ends at 45 degrees.

Assemble the doorframe and clamp it both directions. Drill a pilot hole at each corner of the frame, angling the hole through the top/bottom piece and into the side piece (photo 10). Make sure the hole does not interfere with the rabbet on either piece.

Unclamp the frame pieces, apply glue to the end of each piece, and assemble the frame with a 3-inch wood screw at each joint.

Cut the glazing stops from ⅜ × ⅜-inch stock, mitering each end at 45 degrees. Measure the width and height of the doorframe opening, measuring from rabbet to rabbet. Subtract ⅛ inch from each dimension, then cut the door glazing to this size (see Cutting and Drilling Plastic Glazing on page 35). You will install the glazing after painting or staining the project.

Hang the Door

The door is hung with offset-style hinges (sometimes called institutional hinges) that mount to the hinge cleat on the structure and to the back side of the doorframe. Mount the hinges to the door, about 1¼ inches from the top and bottom edges of the doorframe, using the provided screws.

Position the door so it is centered top-to-bottom over the door opening; it will overlap the opening by about ½ inch at the top and bottom. Fasten the hinges to the hinge cleat with the provided screws (photo 11). Remove the door and hinges for finishing.

Finish the project as desired (see Painting & Staining on pages 39–42 for finishing tips). When the finish is completely dry, fit the glazing into the rabbets of the doorframe and secure it with the glazing stops, nailed at each end and in the center with a 1-inch finish nail. Rehang the door as before.

Learn how to register your Little Free Library on page 156.

Give Box

A give box is one of the simplest and best examples of a community exchange. Anyone can put in anything they want (provided it fits in the box), and anyone can take out anything they want. You can be a giver or a getter, or both, anytime.

Give boxes seem to have origins in Europe, and at least one organization in the United States has formalized the idea to encourage free exchanges of food to help neighbors in need. But regardless of where a give box is planted, if it gets used, you can be sure it's helping someone out.

This version of a give box was adapted from several existing box designs and features an intentionally open interior to accommodate a wide variety of items. One side has two removable shelves; these are optional, and you can add more, if desired. The other side is wide open—a free space for standing up tall items or stacking others. It's even tall enough for hanging up adult-size shirts or jackets.

The roof, side windows, and door all let in natural light so passersby can easily get a hint of what's inside at a glance. The roofing is made from a single panel of clear polycarbonate TwinWall glazing, the same material that's used for the walls and roofs of greenhouses. You can buy it by the sheet at most home centers and some garden stores, and it cuts and drills much like acrylic glazing (which is what the windows and door front are made of, naturally). If you prefer not to have a clear roof, simply use a piece of plywood and cover it with any standard roofing material you like.

INSTRUCTIONS

Cut the Sides, Back, Front, Door, and Shelf Divider

Cut the side, back, and front panels and the door to size using a circular saw or jigsaw. Bevel the top edges of the front and back panels at 14 degrees to follow the roof slope. To mark the angled cuts on the side panels, measure down 4¾ inches from the top rear corner and make a mark along the back edge of the panel. Draw a line from the mark to the top front corner using a straightedge.

Cut the shelf divider and shelves to size. Mark the angled top edge of the shelf divider just as you did with the side panels.

Make the Door and Front-Panel Cutouts

The door and the front panel each get a rectangular cutout made with a jigsaw. Make these cuts carefully

1. Make the door cutout with a jigsaw, using a starter hole to begin each cut.
2. Mark the window cutouts with a pencil compass, or you can trace around any round object that is about 8½" in diameter. 3. Glue and nail the shelf supports to the face of the shelf divider and one of the side panels.

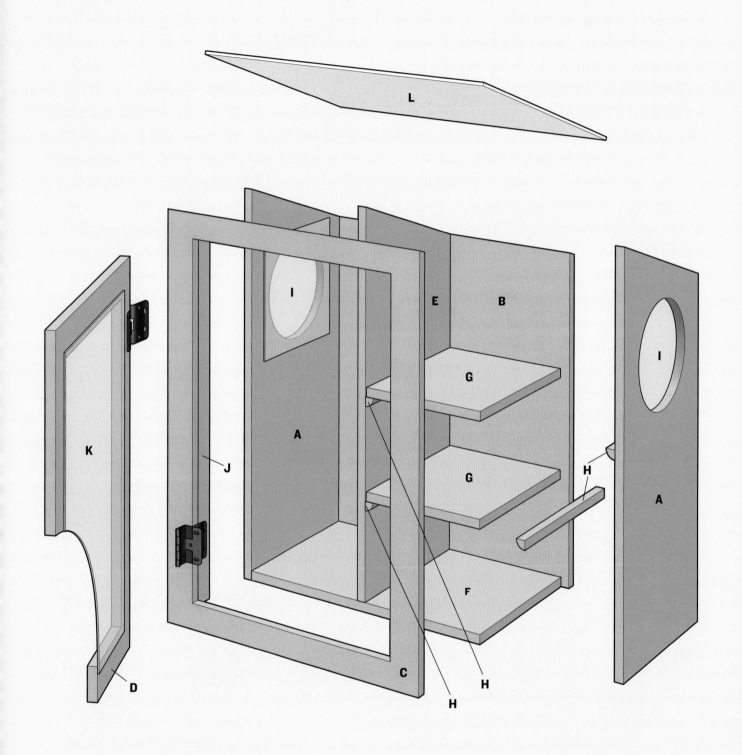

TOOLS & MATERIALS

Circular saw (optional)
Jigsaw
Straightedge
Drill-driver
Drill bits (⅜", ¼", ³⁄₁₆", ⅛")
Pilot-countersink bit
Screwdriver bit
¼" nut driver bit
Framing square
Pencil compass
Screwdriver (optional)
¼" manual nut driver (optional)

Caulking gun
4 × 8' sheet of ¾" plywood
¾ × ¾ × 56" pine quarter-round
  molding
⅛ × 30 × 30" clear acrylic glazing
2 × 2 (nominal) × 29" pine
6mm × 22 × 27" polycarbonate
  TwinWall glazing
55" length of polycarbonate
  U-channel for 6mm TwinWall
  glazing
Waterproof wood glue

(12) 1¼" finish nails
(8) ¾" panhead screws
(54) 1¾" wood screws
(6) #10 × 1½" wood grip screws with
  neoprene washers
(2) exterior offset ("institutional")
  hinges (for ¾" doorframe) with
  screws
Door handle or pull (optional)
Clear silicone caulk
Eye and ear protection
Work gloves

CUTTING LIST

KEY	PART	DIMENSIONS	PCS.	MATERIAL
A	Side panel	¾ × 13½ × 32"	2	Plywood
B	Back panel	¾ × 24 × 27¼"	1	Plywood
C	Front panel	¾ × 24 × 32¼"	1	Plywood
D	Door	¾ × 20 × 29"	1	Plywood
E	Shelf divider	¾ × 13½ × 31¼"	1	Plywood
F	Base	¾ × 13½ × 22½"	1	Plywood
G	Shelf	¾ × 10¾ × 13⅜"	2	Plywood
H	Shelf support	¾ × ¾ × 13½"	4	Quarter-round molding
I	Window glazing	⅛ × 10 × 10"	2	Acrylic glazing
J	Hinge cleat	1½ × 1½ × 29"	1	Pine
K	Door glazing	⅛ × 16 × 25"	1	Acrylic glazing
L	Roofing	6mm × 22" × 27"	1	Polycarbonate glazing
M	U-channel	¹¹⁄₁₆ × 27"	2	Polycarbonate U-channel

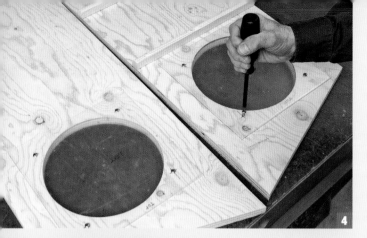

4. Carefully snug the screws to secure the window glazing to the inside faces of the side panels. 5. The front and back panels overlap the edges of the sides and base and fasten to the sides, base, and shelf divider.

using a straightedge guide (see Making Straight Cuts on page 31) if desired so the lines are nice and straight. You will use the cutout material for the base of the box and the shelves.

Draw a 19 × 28-inch rectangle on the back side of the front panel. Center the rectangle so it is 2½ inches from each side edge and 2 inches from the top and bottom edges. Drill a ⅜-inch-diameter starter hole (see Making Curves and Interior Cutouts on page 32) at each corner of the rectangle. Use the jigsaw to cut between the starter holes to complete the cutout.

Repeat the same process to complete the door cutout, marking a rectangle that is 15 × 24 inches, centered so it is 2½ inches from each of the four edges (photo 1).

Cut the Base and Shelves

Cut the box base to size using the plywood cutout from the front panel. Cut the shelves to size using the cutout material from the door.

Cut the Side Windows

Mark a vertical centerline on the inside face of each side panel, about 7 inches from the top edge. Measure up 22½ inches from the bottom edge of the panel and make a cross mark on the vertical centerline. This marks the centerpoint of the window cutout.

Draw an 8½-inch-diameter circle around the centerpoint using a pencil compass (photo 2). Drill a ⅜-inch starter hole inside the marked circle and complete the cutout with a jigsaw.

Install the Shelf Supports

Mark one side of the shelf divider and the inside face of one of the side panels for positioning the shelf supports; the shelves can go on either side of the box. You can also position the shelves at any height you like. As shown, the shelves are about 8 inches and 16¼ inches from the bottom of the box interior.

Measure up from the bottom end of the shelf divider and mark the height for each shelf. Use a framing square (or a small square and a straightedge) to draw a horizontal line at each shelf mark; these lines represent the bottom edges of the shelves.

Create the same lines on the side panel, but add ¾ inch to each shelf height; this is because the side panel will overlap the base of the box, so its bottom edge will sit ¾ inch lower than the shelf divider.

Cut the four shelf supports to length from quarter-round molding using a jigsaw. Drill three pilot holes through each shelf support. Apply wood glue to one of the flat faces of each support and position the support so the other flat face is on one of the marked lines on the shelf divider or side panel. Fasten each support with three 1¼-inch finish nails (photo 3).

Add the Window Glazing

Cut the windows to size using a jigsaw with a fine-tooth metal- or plastic-cutting blade (see Cutting and Drilling Plastic Glazing on page 35 for tips on cutting and drilling acrylic glazing). Mark a hole for drilling at each corner of the glazing, measuring 1½ inches from the side and top/bottom edges. Place the glazing over a sacrificial board and drill a ³⁄₁₆-inch hole through the glazing at each mark. The holes should be slightly larger than the threaded portion of the ¾-inch panhead screws.

Lay each side panel on a flat surface with its inside face up. Remove the protective plastic from one face of each glazing piece and place the uncovered face over the window hole in the side panel, so the glazing is centered over the hole side to side and top to bottom. Fasten the glazing to the panel with four ¾-inch panhead screws (photo 4). Be careful to drive the screws just snug; if they're too tight, they might crack the glazing.

Assemble the Box

Mark layout lines for the shelf divider onto the inside faces of the front and back panels: Measure over from one side edge of the front/back panel and make marks at 11⅝ inches and 12⅜ inches. Make a set of marks near the top and bottom edges of each piece.

Apply glue to both side edges of the base. Fit the side panels over the base so they are flush with the base at the front and rear. Fasten through each side and into the base with three 1¾-inch wood screws.

Glue the rear edges of the side panels and the base. Fit the back panel over the edges of the sides and base so all pieces are flush at the outside. Fasten the back to the sides and base with four 1¾-inch screws in each edge.

Make three evenly spaced marks (from top to bottom) on the back side of the back panel, 12 inches from either side edge. Apply glue to the rear edge of the shelf divider. Place the divider on the base and against the back panel, aligning the divider between its layout marks on the back panel. Drive three 1¾-inch screws through the back panel and into the divider, placing a screw at each mark on the back panel.

Glue the front edges of the side panels and base. Apply a line of glue between the marks on the inside face of the front panel. Fit the front panel over the box so all pieces are flush on the outside and top, and the divider is in between its layout marks (photo 5). Fasten the front panel with four 1¾-inch screws into the side panels and base. Also drive two screws into the divider through the panel, about 1 inch each from the top or bottom of the front panel.

Add the Hinge Cleat

Cut the 2 × 2 hinge cleat to length. Apply glue to one face of the cleat and position it against the inside of the front panel so it is flush with the edge of the door opening. Fasten the cleat with three 1¾-inch screws.

Prepare the Roofing

Cut the polycarbonate roofing to size using a jigsaw with the same blade used for the acrylic glazing. You can also use a circular saw with a hollow-ground panel blade with 10 to 12 teeth per inch. Cut the panel with the same basic techniques used for cutting the glazing. Note that the lines in the panel will run parallel to the sides of the box when the roofing is installed.

Cut the two pieces of polycarbonate U-channel to length with a jigsaw. Fit pieces of U-channel over the front and rear edges of the roofing panel so they are flush at both sides. The U-channel keeps bugs and rain or snow out of the hollow cells of the roofing material.

Drill three ⅛-inch holes through the bottom U-channel, aligning each hole with one of the hollow cells in the roofing. These are weep holes that will allow condensation to drain from the cells.

Install the Roofing

Set the roofing panel on the assembled box so it overhangs about 4 inches at the front of the box and equally at both sides. Drill a ¼-inch pilot hole through the roofing near each corner of the box, about 1½ inches from the front and rear faces. The holes are slightly larger than the screw shank to provide room for expansion of the plastic roofing.

6. Drive the roofing screws so the neoprene washer is slightly compressed, creating a waterproof seal around the screw. 7. Center the glazing over the back side of the door so it overlaps the door cutout equally on all sides.

8. Screw the door hinges into the edge of the front-panel cutout. 9. Caulk along the edges of the door and window cutouts to seal the glazing to the plywood edges. This caulk goes on white but will be clear after it dries.

Be careful to drill just through the roofing and no more than about ⅛ inch into the plywood; if you drill too deep, the screws won't hold. Also make sure the holes go through the hollow part of cell and not into a cell wall.

Drill two more pilot holes over the shelf divider, about 1½ inches from the front and rear of the box.

Fasten the roofing to the side panels and shelf divider with six #10 × 1½-inch wood grip screws driven through the pilot holes. Drive the screws so they are snug to the panel and the neoprene washer under the screw head is slightly compressed—but not more (photo 6). You can drive them with a drill-driver and ¼-inch nut driver tip, but be careful not to drive too far, which can crack the panel. Alternatively, use a manual nut driver to tighten the screws snug.

Add the Door Glazing
It's best to install the door glazing and hang the door, then remove both for the finishing process.

Cut the door glazing to size using a jigsaw, as with the window glazing. Mark three pilot hole locations along each edge of the glazing, ¼ inch from the outside edge. Place one hole about 1½ inches from each corner and one hole centered in between.

Place the glazing face down onto a sacrificial surface (leaving the protective film in place, as applicable). Drill a ³⁄₁₆-inch pilot hole at each mark.

Place the door face down on your worksurface. Center the glazing over the door so it overlaps the door cutout by ½ inch on all sides (photo 7). Fasten the glazing to the door with twelve ¾-inch panhead screws, being careful not to overtighten the screws so you don't crack the glazing.

Hang the Door
Mount the door hinges to the back side of the door using the provided screws. Position the hinges 3 inches from the top and bottom of the door. You can make the door swing either way, depending on which side you mount the hinges.

Mount the door to the front panel, screwing into the side edge of the door cutout with 1¾-inch wood screws (photo 8). The screws that come with hinges usually are too short for getting a good grip in plywood edges. The door should overlap the cutout equally at the top and bottom.

Finish the Project
Remove the door from the box, then remove the hinges and the door glazing and window glazing. Keep the hardware in a safe place for re-installation later.

Apply an exterior finish to the outside of the box and to all surfaces of the door. If you use a stain or clear coat finish, it will look best if you leave the plywood edges exposed, lending a modern look that goes well with the polycarbonate roofing. Alternatively, if you'd like to paint your project, you can create the appearance of a seamless box by covering the plywood edges with auto body filler before painting.

After the finish has fully cured, reinstall the door glazing, then mount the door hinges and hang the door. Install a door handle or pull, as desired. Add the shelves by setting them on the shelf supports. Finally, seal around the window and door cutouts with a fine bead of clear silicone caulk (photo 9). Let the caulk cure overnight before installing or using the box.

Learn how to register your Little Free Library on page 156.

Kitchen Cabinet Upcycle

One of the easiest things to upcycle, or repurpose, into a tiny structure is an old kitchen cabinet with doors. A cabinet is a complete six-sided wood box and needs little more than a roof and a good slathering of protective finish to be ready for outdoor duty. Almost any small- to medium-size cabinet will do, but it's usually best to use a wall cabinet, as opposed to a base cabinet. Wall cabinets tend to be a more manageable size and have a more finished look—without the deep recess and toe-kick space at the bottom that base cabinets have.

You can also use different shapes of cabinets, and the instructions here teach you how to build a custom roof to fit any cabinet box. It's a bonus if the cabinet has traditional frame-and-panel doors, with a wood panel captured inside a solid-wood frame. This may sound high-end and is often found on better-quality cabinets, but it's also a common feature of builder-grade cabinets (usually made of oak) sold off the shelf at home centers. The nice thing about the frame-and-panel doors is that you can easily remove the panels (they're not glued in place) and replace them with clear acrylic glazing to make see-through doors.

The most important rule about cabinet structures is that you must finish them—but good! Cabinet boxes (every part except the face frame and doors) are typically made of particleboard—a nice, flat, smooth material when it's dry, but if it gets wet, it swells up and eventually falls apart. And don't be fooled by the "wood look" on the cabinet panels; these are just particleboard covered with a thin layer of melamine plastic. Give everything a complete coating of exterior paint to protect it from moisture.

The project as shown has standard three-tab "asphalt," or composition, shingles for roofing. It requires only five shingles for the entire roof, so this is a good option if you have some leftover shingles around the house (new shingles are usually sold in bundles of 22 shingles; way more than you need). Otherwise, any alternative roofing material will do.

Note: The cabinet shown here required a few additional pieces for reinforcement and aesthetics. These include ¼-inch plywood side panels (for looks and additional weather protection), a reinforcing back panel of ⅝-inch plywood (the cabinet had only a thin hardboard back), and reinforcing strips of ⅝-inch plywood at the top and bottom (to stiffen

1. Use a straightedge to experiment with different roof slopes and mark the slope for each side of the roof. 2. Drive screws through the gable nailers and into the center (of the thickness) of the cabinet edges. 3. Install the gables so they overlap the front and back of the cabinet and are flush at the top with the cabinet's corners.

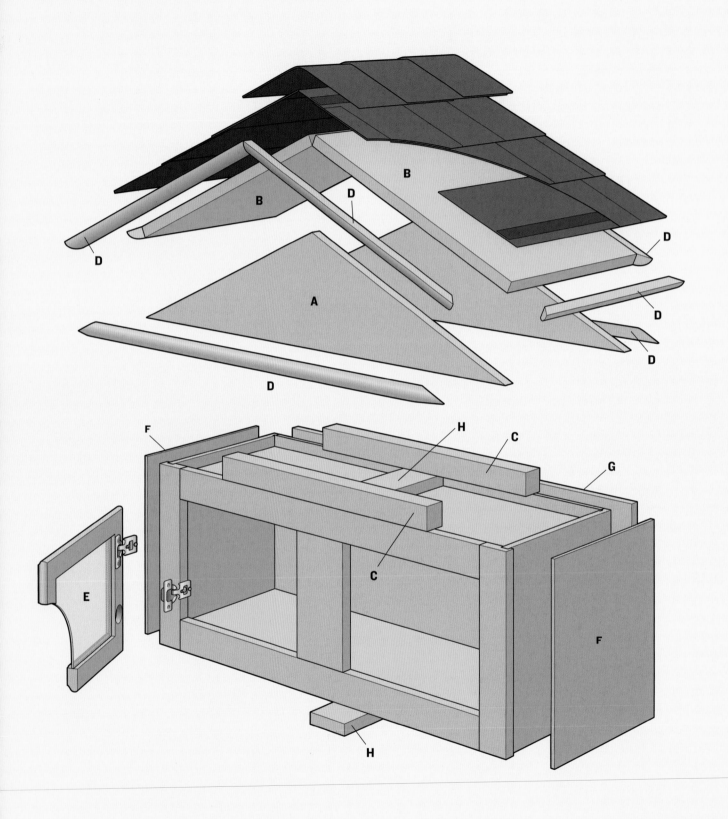

TOOLS & MATERIALS

Straightedge
Square
Circular saw or jigsaw
Drill-driver
Pilot-countersink bit
Screwdriver bit
Miter saw, miter box, or handsaw
Utility knife
Caulking gun

Wall cabinet
4 × 4' sheet of ¾" plywood
2 × 2 (nominal) × 8' pine
(2) ¾ × ¾ × 96" quarter-round
  molding
⅛" acrylic glazing (optional; size as
  needed to fit doors)
(5) 3-tab (flat) composition roofing
  shingles (approx. 12 × 36")

(8) 2½" wood screws
(24) 2" wood screws
(32) 1½" finish nails
(38) 1¼" roofing nails
Waterproof wood glue
Clear silicone caulk (optional)
Eye and ear protection
Work gloves

CUTTING LIST

KEY	PART	DIMENSIONS	PCS.	MATERIAL
A	Gable	¾" × cut to fit	2	Plywood
B	Roof deck	¾" × cut to fit	2	Plywood
C	Nailer	1½ × 1½" × cut to fit	2	Pine
D	Trim	¾ × ¾" × cut to fit	8	Quarter-round molding
E	Door glazing	⅛" × cut to fit	2	Acrylic glazing
F	Side cladding	¼" × cut to fit	2	Plywood or siding
G	Back cladding	⅝" × cut to fit	1	Plywood or siding
H	Stiffener	⅝ × 3" × cut to fit	2	Plywood

the cabinet box and provide more support where the bottom will mount to a post). Your cabinet may or may not need similar or other additions; they are merely shown here as an example and are not included in the project steps.

INSTRUCTIONS

Lay out the Roof

A traditional gable roof is easy to build and can be customized with any slope, or steepness, you like. Use a half-sheet of ¾-inch plywood as a drawing board to lay out the roof for your cabinet. You will cut the roof parts from the same plywood, but at this stage you're just laying out the shape of the roof and finding its dimensions.

Draw a straight line across the face of the plywood using a straightedge. Mark the center of the line, then use a square to draw a perpendicular line at the mark. Place the cabinet on its back over the plywood so the top edge of the cabinet overhangs the line by ½ inch and the cabinet box is centered side to side over the perpendicular line.

Position the straightedge so it touches the cabinet top and intersects the perpendicular line. The straightedge represents one side of the gable roof. Experiment with different roof slopes to find what you like. Draw an angled line along the bottom edge of the straightedge to define the roof slope. Draw a matching line on the other side of the roof so the lines create a symmetrical triangle (photo 1). The resulting point at the top is the roof peak. In the project shown, the roof measures about 7 inches from the baseline to the peak.

Cut the Gables

Remove the cabinet from the plywood. Measure the laid-out triangle and draw the same triangle along the edge of the plywood panel. **Tip:** You can avoid the long straight cut by laying out the triangle along one of the panel's factory edges. Cut out the gable with a circular saw or jigsaw.

Using the cut gable as a template, trace around its perimeter to mark the cutting lines for the second gable, then cut out the second gable.

4. Position all roof deck trim so the rounded side of the molding faces out.
5. Cut the horizontal trim to fit the gable slope, then bevel the cut for a finished look.

Install the Nailers

Cut the two 2 × 2 nailers about 12 inches shorter than the width of the cabinet. The nailers provide backing for fastening the gables, but their edges should not stick up above the top sloping edges of the gable. If your roof has a very low slope, you may need to make your nailers a bit shorter; if your roof is steep, you can make the nailers a bit longer.

Position a nailer onto the front edge of the cabinet box so it is centered side to side on the cabinet and the front face of the nailer is flush with front of the cabinet. Drill four pilot holes (see Screwing and Nailing in Wood on page 33) through the nailer and into the top edge of the cabinet.

Apply wood glue to the top edge of the cabinet face frame in the area where the nailer will go. Reposition the nailer and fasten it to the cabinet with four 2½-inch wood screws (photo 2). Repeat the same process to install the other nailer at the rear of the cabinet, so the outside face of the nailer is flush with the back of the cabinet.

Install the Gables

Set the cabinet on its back. Apply glue to the front edge of the front nailer. Position one of the gables over the cabinet so its bottom edge overlaps the top of the cabinet by ½ inch (as you did with the gable layout) and it is precisely centered side to side. The sloping top edges of the gable should just cover the top corners of the cabinet (photo 3). This ensures that the area under the roof will be enclosed once the roof deck panels are installed.

Fasten the gable to the nailer with four 2-inch screws. Flip the cabinet onto its front side and install the second gable at the back using the same techniques.

Cut and Install the Roof Decks

Measure the distance between the outside faces of the two gables, measuring straight across the top from front to back; use this dimension for the width of the roof deck panels. Measure from the peak of each gable to the point at the bottom end; use this dimension for the length of the roof decks. Cut the two roof deck panels to size.

Apply glue to the top edges of the gables. Position the roof deck panels on the gables so the roof decks meet at the peak (there will be a gap at the top corners of the roof decks; this will be covered later with roofing) and all the pieces are flush at the front and rear. Fasten the roof decks to the gables with four 2-inch screws along each edge.

Trim the Roof Decking

Use quarter-round molding to cover the exposed edges of the roof decking. It looks best to miter the ends of the trim at the corners, and you may have to make a few test cuts to get the angles right. Make the cuts with a miter saw or miter box, or simply with a handsaw, following a cutting line.

Start with the pieces covering the front and rear edges of the roof decking; the miter angles at the top are based on the shape of your roof. Make test cuts to find the right angle, then cut the top end of each trim piece using that angle. Cut the bottom end of each piece at 45 degrees. Apply glue to the front and rear edges of the roof deck and install the trim so it is flush with the top faces of the roof decking. The round side of the trim should face out; the flat sides go against the plywood and face up, respectively. Tack each piece of trim in place with four 1½-inch finish nails.

Cut two more pieces of trim to cover the bottom edges of the roof decking, mitering each end at 45 degrees so the pieces meet the gable trim at the corners. Install each piece with glue and three 1½-inch finish nails (photo 4).

Add the Horizontal Trim

The front and back sides of the cabinet get horizontal pieces of quarter-round that meet the angled gable trim. At the front of the cabinet, the horizontal trim serves as a drip cap (see Ready for Rain on page 29) over the door. The joint where the horizontal and sloping trim meet is a tricky one, given the acute angle and the rounded shape of the molding. To simplify the cut on the horizontal trim, make a sharp miter cut that follows the sloping trim pieces, then bevel the end so that it tapers down to the gable panel, or you can make your own custom cut as desired.

Cut the horizontal trim for the front and rear of the cabinet so that one flat side of the molding is flush with the bottom edge of the gable panel and the other flat side is against the gable panel (photo 5). The rounded side faces out. Install the trim with glue and 1¼-inch finish nails.

Install the Starter Shingles

Starter shingles are partial-width shingles installed along the bottom edge of the roof. They are covered by, and prop up, the first row of exposed shingles to establish the stepped pattern, and they cover the gaps between the tabs of the first-row shingles.

Place a full three-tab shingle flat on a cutting surface (such as scrap plywood). Using a straightedge and utility knife, cut off the three tabs at the top of the tab notches, yielding an approximately 7-inch-wide × 36-inch-long strip; you don't need the tabs. The cut should be about 1 inch away from the adhesive strip on the top surface of the shingle.

Cut the strip into two pieces that are about ½ inch longer than the width of the roof decking. Position one of the cut pieces along the bottom of one roof plane so the cut edge of the shingle overhangs the bottom and side edges of the roof deck by about ¼ inch. The adhesive strip should be near the bottom edge of the roof. Nail the shingle in place with three 1¼-inch roofing nails driven about 3 inches up from the bottom edge (photo 6). Install the other starter shingle on the other side of the roof.

Install the Remaining Shingles

Cut eight (or as many as needed for your roof) pieces of shingle to equal the roof width plus ½ inch. For each piece, measure from one of the factory side edges of the shingle, and make the cut near the center of the shingle's length. These are full-width shingles; you don't cut down the width as with the starter shingles. If the roof is narrow enough, you can get two pieces from each full three-tab shingle.

Place the first cut shingle over the starter shingle on one side of the roof so the bottom and side edges of the shingles are flush. Nail the top shingle with three roofing nails, just below the adhesive strip and above the tab slots on the shingles.

6. Install each starter shingle so it overhangs the decking by about ¼" and the adhesive strip is near the bottom (eave) edge of the roof. 7. Nail the shingles just above the level of the tab slots so the nails are covered by the next row of shingle.

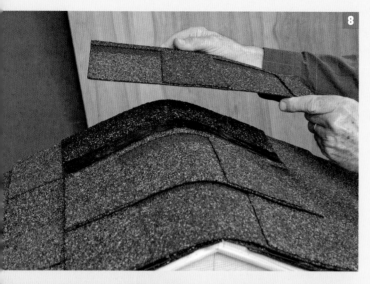

Place the next shingle over the first full-width shingle so the tab slots are offset by about half a tab's width. Overlap the first shingle to the tops of the tab slots. Nail the second shingle with three nails, as with the first.

Repeat the same process to install two more shingles, offsetting the tab slots with each new row (photo 7). Trim the top shingle along the roof peak. Install the remaining shingles on the other side of the roof using the same techniques.

Add the Ridge-Cap Shingles

Cut a full shingle into thirds along the tab lines to create three 12 × 12-inch pieces; these are the ridge caps. Wrap the first cap over the roof peak so it covers the top shingles equally on both sides of the roof and the finished edge of the cap is flush with the shingles at the front. Nail the cap with one nail at each side, just in front of the adhesive strip.

Place another cap piece onto the ridge, overlapping the first cap as with the other shingles. Nail the second cap in place. Fit the last cap in place and mark it at the rear roof edge. Trim the cap at the marks using a utility knife, then install the last shingle with four nails, one near each corner. Make sure the nails go into the roof decking and not the trim molding.

Remove the Door Panels

The remaining steps are optional and apply only to cabinets with frame-and-panel doors. This type of door typically has a solid-hardwood frame and a separate wood panel that is held in place by channels in the edges of the frame pieces. To modify the doors for glazing, you can cut out the back portion of the channel to remove the panel, then cut glazing to fit in the frame. If you don't want glazed doors, or if your cabinet doesn't have frame-and-panel doors, you can skip right to finishing your project.

To remove the door panels, first remove the doors by separating the door-half of each hinge from the cabinet-half of the hinge. Cabinet hinges usually include two pieces that can be separated by pressing a spring tab or removing a screw or two.

Lay each door face down. Slip a piece of paper between the back of the door panel and the hardwood frame until

8. Trim the last cap piece so it is flush with the roof edge. 9. Make several passes with a utility knife to cut out the back lip of the doorframe channel. 10. Apply a continuous bead of caulk around the glazing, sealing it against the wood frame.

the paper stops in the bottom of the channel. Mark a line on the paper along the edge of the frame, then pull out the paper. This tells you how deep the channels are.

Using the marked paper as a guide, draw lines along the side and bottom edges of the frame, indicating the depth of the channels. Cut along these lines with a utility knife (use a new blade), making multiple passes until you cut through the lip that creates the back of the channel (photo 9). This frees up the edges of the door panel along the sides and bottom of the frame. If you can remove the panel, you can leave the top channel intact; if you can't remove the panel, cut out the back of the top channel as well, then remove the door panel.

Cut and Install the Door Glazing

Cut two pieces of acrylic glazing to the same size as the wood door panels (see Cutting and Drilling Plastic Glazing on page 35 for help with cutting acrylic glazing). This should leave about 1/16 inch of space around the perimeter of the glazing, for expansion. Fit each piece of glazing into the channels of a doorframe. Caulk along the perimeter of the glazing to secure the edges to the frame (photo 10). Let the caulk cure overnight.

If you're ready to apply a finish to your project, you can leave the doors off for the finishing process. To reinstall the doors, fit the hinge halves back together, securing them with the tabs or screws, as applicable.

Tool Booth

The Tool Booth is a freestanding structure that's sized for long-handled tools, like rakes, shovels, and hoes. A similar design in Britain might be called a sentry shed, owing to the resemblance to a sentry box or guardhouse. (It's too small to be an outhouse, so you don't have to worry about that association.) This project is easy to build (especially with a helper) and works equally well for personal storage in a backyard garden and for open exchange in a more public location.

The structure measures just over 2 × 2 feet on the outside and stands a little over 6 feet tall. The interior space is wide open, but you can easily add a stack of shelves running up one of the corners for all manner of small items or install vertical dividers to organize standing tools and long hanging items.

The basic box structure of the Tool Booth is built with two sheets of plywood and a few pieces of construction lumber. To complete the project as shown, you'll use some 1× (¾-inch-thick) lumber to trim the corners of the box and the roof edges and to create the Z-bracing on the front side of the door. The roofing shown here is made with cedar siding, but if you like, you can substitute any suitable roofing or siding material of your choice.

To protect the box from prolonged exposure to moisture (such as through soil contact), the Tool Booth has a base made of PT lumber, and the base extends 1 inch below the box. For protection from surface water and to ensure the structure stands straight and tall for many years, place the Tool Booth on a level foundation of gravel or stones (see Freestanding Structures on page 145).

INSTRUCTIONS

Cut the Box Parts

Cut the side panels, front panel, back panel, floor, and roof deck pieces to size using a circular saw or jigsaw. If desired, use a straightedge guide (see Making Straight Cuts on page 31) to ensure straight cuts. To mark the triangular top ends of the front and back panels, first mark the center (side to side) at the top of each panel. Then, make a mark 12 inches down each side edge. Draw a diagonal line connecting each side mark with the center mark. The angle at the peak is 45 degrees.

1. Hold the pencil straight up and down while rotating the compass to draw the top of the door. 2. Cut along the inside edge of the door outline using a jigsaw. 3. Drive the roof deck screws along the reference lines so the screws are centered over the front and back panels.

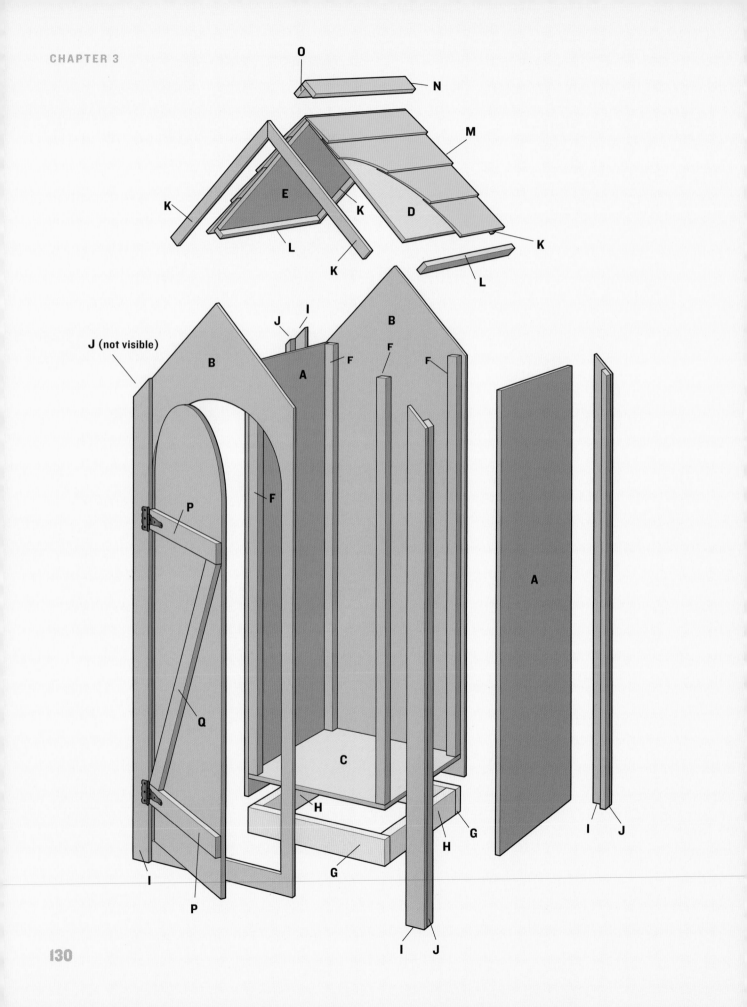

TOOLS & MATERIALS

Circular saw (optional)
Jigsaw
Straightedge
Paint stir stick or flat stick (approx. 12" long)
Drill-driver
Drill bits (1/16", 3/8")
Pilot-countersink bit
Screwdriver bit
Hammer

Miter saw or miter box
Thin tapered wood shims (optional)
(2) 4 × 8' sheets of 5/8" plywood
(4) 2 × 2 (nominal) × 8' pine
2 × 4 (nominal) × 8' PT pine
(5) 1 × 3 (nominal) × 8' pine
(5) 1 × 2 (nominal) × 8' pine
(2) 11/16 × 8" (nominal) × 10' beveled cedar siding
(8) 3½" wood screws

(93) 1½" wood screws
(20) 1⅛" wood screws
(72) 2¼" finish nails
(48) 1¼" finish nails
Waterproof wood glue
(2) exterior door or gate hinges with screws
Exterior door or gate latch (optional)
Eye and ear protection
Work gloves

CUTTING LIST

KEY	PART	DIMENSIONS	PCS.	MATERIAL
A	Side panel	5/8 × 22¾ × 60"	2	Plywood
B	Front/back panel	5/8 × 24 × 72"	2	Plywood
C	Floor	5/8 × 22¾ × 22¾"	1	Plywood
D	Roof deck—right	5/8 × 22 × 27"	1	Plywood
E	Roof deck—left	5/8 × 21⅜ × 27"	1	Plywood
F	Corner post	1½ × 1½ × 56⅞"	4	Pine
G	Base front/rear	1½ × 3½ × 22¾"	2	PT pine
H	Base sides	1½ × 3½ × 19¾"	2	PT pine
I	Corner trim—front/rear	¾ × 2½" × cut to fit	4	Pine
J	Corner trim—side	¾ × 1½" × cut to fit	4	Pine
K	Roof gable trim	¾ × 1½ × 22¾"	4	Pine
L	Roof eave trim	¾ × 1½ × 27"	2	Pine
M	Roofing	11/16 × 7⅛ × 29"	8	Cedar siding
N	Roof cap—right	¾ × 2½ × 29"	1	Cedar
O	Roof cap—left	¾ × 1½ × 29"	1	Cedar
P	Z-brace—horizontal	¾ × 2½ × 20¼"	2	Pine
Q	Z-brace—diagonal	¾ × 2½" × cut to fit	1	Pine

4. Slide the base into the bottom of the box until it contacts the corner posts. 5. Install the front and rear trim with glue and nails, overlapping the edges of the side trim pieces. 6. Install the roof trim to cover the edges of the roof decking. All roof trims should be flush with the top of the decking. 7. Nail the roofing boards where they overlap to prevent the nails from penetrating all the way through the roof deck.

Mark the Door Cutout

The door is made from the piece you remove when you cut the door opening. It has a rounded top that you draw with a homemade compass.

Mark a rectangle on the front panel so its edges are 1¾ inches from the side edges, 2½ inches from the bottom edge, and 12 inches from the top edge. Make a short vertical line marking the center of the panel, about 10 inches from the top edge of the rectangle. Make a short horizontal line 10¼

inches from the top of the rectangle, intersecting the vertical centerline; this indicates the pivot point for the compass.

To make a homemade compass, drill a ¹⁄₁₆-inch hole through the center of a paint stir stick (or similar flat stick), about 1 inch from one end of the stick. Drill a second hole 10¼ inches from the first.

Insert a small finish nail through one of the holes, then tap the nail into the pivot-point marking on the front panel so the stick is flat against the panel. Insert the tip of a pencil into the other hole in the compass. Rotate the compass to draw the top of the door; it will make a 20½-inch-diameter semicircle (photo 1).

Cut Out the Door

Mark the position for a starter hole (see Making Curves and Interior Cutouts on page 32) for the jigsaw blade, 6 inches up from the bottom right corner of the door outline. Drill a ⅜-inch-diameter starter hole at the mark so the hole is inside the door outline and just touches the line. When viewed from the front, the starter hole will be at the lower left of the door but will be hidden from the outside by the door's Z-bracing.

Insert the blade of a jigsaw into the starter hole and complete the door cutout, staying on the *inside* edge of the door outline (photo 2). The 1/16 inch to 1/8 inch of material removed by the jigsaw blade will create an even gap all the way around the door.

Install the Corner Posts

Cut the four corner posts to length using a jigsaw or circular saw. Apply glue to one face of each corner post and position it along one side edge of a side panel, flush with the edge and top of the panel. Fasten the post through the outside of the panel using five 1½-inch screws. The bottom of the post should be 3⅛ inches from the bottom edge of the panel.

Assemble the Box

Lay one of the side panels flat so the corner posts are facing up. Apply glue to the outside face of one of the corner posts and to the adjacent plywood edge. Fit the back panel against the glued surfaces so the panels are flush at the bottom and outside corner. The back panel completely covers the edge of the side panel.

Fasten the back panel to the corner post with five 1½-inch screws, driving through the outside face of the back panel. Repeat the same process to join the back panel to the other side panel, then install the front panel. The corner posts at the front will extend into the door opening about ⅜ inch on each side. The exposed portions of the posts will serve as stops for the door.

Draw guidelines for screws along both sides of each roof deck piece, 1¹³/₁₆ inches in from the side edge. Apply glue to the top edges of the front and back panels on the left side of the roof. Fit the left side roof deck panel onto the glued edges so it stops at the peak of the roof and overhangs the front and back panels equally on both

sides. Fasten the deck to the edges of the front and back panels with four 1½-inch screws along each edge, driving the screws along the guidelines.

Repeat the same process to install the right roof deck panel so it overlaps the top edge of the left deck panel. Fasten to the front and back panels, as before, and add two screws through the right deck panel and into the edge of the left deck panel (photo 3).

Build the Base

Cut the four base pieces to length using a circular saw or jigsaw. Apply glue to the ends of the base side (19¾-inch-long) pieces. Fit the base front and rear pieces over the sides to form a square assembly. Fasten each joint through the front/rear piece with two 3½-inch screws.

Apply glue to the top edges of the base assembly. Position the plywood floor on the base so all four edges are flush at the outside of the base. Fasten through the floor and into the base with twelve 1½-inch screws, placing one screw near each corner and two screws evenly spaced in between.

Install the Base

Lay the box assembly on its back. Apply glue to the inside faces of the side, front, and rear panels, in the areas below

8. Align the straightedge with the edge of the horizontal brace and mark the diagonal brace.

9. Install the door by mounting the hinges to the horizontal Z-braces and the front corner trim piece.

the bottom ends of the corner posts. Fit the base into the bottom of the box so the longer (front and rear) base pieces face the front and rear of the box (photo 4). Push in the base until it hits the corner posts, tapping it with a hammer, if necessary. The base should extend about 1 inch below the bottom edges of the box.

Drive three 1½-inch screws through each of the side and back panels and into the base, about 1¼ inches from the bottom edges of the panels. Drive one screw through the front panel at each side of the door opening.

Add the Corner Trim

All of the corner trim pieces are cut individually to fit the box. The side pieces get 45-degree bevel cuts at their top ends; the front and rear pieces get 45-degree miter cuts at their top ends. It's easiest to make the 45-degree cuts first, leaving the pieces a little long. Then, fit each piece in place on the box and mark where to make the bottom cut for the overall length. You can install the trim pieces with the box lying down or standing up, whichever is easier.

Make the 45-degree bevel cut at the top end of each side trim piece using a miter saw or miter box. Position each piece at one of the box corners so the beveled end butts up against the roof deck and the side edge is flush with the outside face

of the front or rear panel. Mark the trim piece to length so the end will be even with the bottom of the box. Remove the trim and square-cut its bottom end at the mark.

Apply glue to the inside (1½-inch-wide) face of each side trim piece and install it onto one of the side panels with six 2¼-inch finish nails. The outside edge of the trim should be flush with the face of the front/rear panel of the box.

Cut and install the front and rear corner trim pieces using the same techniques. The front and rear trims overlap the edges of the side trims (photo 5).

Add the Roof Trim

Cut the roof eave trim pieces to length, square-cutting each end. Install each piece along the bottom edge of a roof deck panel using glue and four 2¼-inch finish nails. The trim should be flush with the side edges and top faces of the roof decking.

Cut the roof gable trim pieces to length, mitering the top ends at 45 degrees. Install them with glue and four 2¼-inch nails each so they meet at the peak of the roof, are flush with the top faces of the roof deck, and cover the ends of the eave trim (photo 6).

Install the Roofing

Cut the eight roofing boards to length using a circular saw or jigsaw. Apply glue to the back side of one of the boards, staying about 1 inch away from the ends and bottom edge. Position the board on one side of the roof, overhanging the eave trim by about ½ inch and overhanging the front and rear gable trim by about ¼ inch. Nail through the roofing board and into the eave trim with six 1¼-inch finish nails.

To install the next roofing board above the first, apply a straight line of glue on the back side of the second piece, about ½ inch from the bottom and top edges. Fit the board onto the roof so it overlaps the first board by 1 inch. Drive five 1¼-inch finish nails through the second board, through the first board, and into the roof decking, keeping the nails about ½ inch from the bottom edge of the second board.

Note: The trick to nailing the roofing is to prevent the nails from poking through the underside of the roof deck. If you see any nail points coming through, adjust your nailing position or use shorter nails. Also, if you see any splitting of the roofing boards, drill ⅟₁₆-inch pilot holes for the nails.

Repeat the same process to install one more full-width roofing board. Rip-cut the fourth roofing board to width so its top edge is aligned with the peak of the roof. Install the fourth piece as with the other three, leaving the top edge unfastened (photo 7).

Add the Roof Cap
Cut the roof cap pieces to length. Apply glue to one edge of the left (1½-inch-wide) cap piece. Fit the right (2½-inch-wide) cap piece over the glued edge, forming an L-shaped angle. Fasten the pieces together with four 1½-inch screws.

Position the cap on the roof peak so it lies flat over both sides and is flush with the ends of the roofing boards. Fasten the cap to the roof deck with four 1½-inch screws on each side.

Install the Door Z-Bracing
Cut the two horizontal Z-bracing boards to length. **Note:** The length of these boards should equal the door's width; if necessary, adjust the dimensions as needed.

Mark horizontal reference lines on the front face of the door, 5 inches and 42½ inches from the bottom edge. Apply glue to one face of one of the Z-brace boards. Place the board on the door so its bottom edge is on one of the reference lines. Clamp the board in place, then flip the door over and drive three pairs of 1⅛-inch screws through the door and into the Z-brace. Repeat with the other Z-brace.

Lay the door flat with its front facing up. Set the diagonal Z-brace board over the horizontal braces so the right-side edge of the diagonal brace meets the right end of the top horizontal brace and the left-side edge of the diagonal board meets the left end of the bottom horizontal brace. Place a straightedge or square over the diagonal board, aligned with the bottom edge of the top horizontal brace, and mark a line across the diagonal board (photo 8). Do the same at the bottom horizontal brace, aligning the straightedge with the top edge of the brace.

Cut the diagonal brace at the marked lines. Apply glue to its back side and clamp it to the front of the door so it meets flush with the horizontal braces. Fasten the diagonal brace through the back side of the door with four pairs of 1⅛-inch screws.

Hang the Door
Lay the box on its back. Set the door into its opening so the gaps around the door are even at both sides and the top. If desired, slip thin wood shims (or folded-up paper) into the gaps so the door doesn't move. Install the door with two outdoor hinges using the provided screws or bolts (photo 9). Install a latch on the door, as desired.

Installing Your Structure

There are many ways to mount a tiny structure, and really no rules—unless the city or your HOA imposes some. Make sure you check for any potential restrictions or requirements that may affect where and how you install your structure (see Location, Permission & Other Considerations on page 15).

The most common method of installing a structure intended for community sharing is to mount it on a wood post buried in the ground. The post goes in just like a fencepost and usually doesn't need to be anchored in concrete; compacted soil or rock gives an average-size structure plenty of stability.

The next question is how to attach the post to the structure. There are two easy options. One is to build a simple platform using wood cut from the post and a short piece of board lumber. The other is to use a metal post base that fastens to the top of the post and the bottom of the structure. This chapter teaches both methods, as well as how to bury the post for a secure installation.

Of course, a post isn't the only means for mounting something off the ground. A stout, mature tree in the right location works just as well (and you won't have to dig a hole), as does an existing fencepost. There are some rules to putting hardware into trees to minimize damage, so be sure to take these into consideration. Fences are more straightforward, but you want to choose a strong post that's well anchored in the ground, lest your fence start to list.

Some structures stand on the ground rather than on top of posts. These simply need a solid, well-draining foundation of gravel, stone, or concrete block. This keeps the structure level through the changing seasons and helps prevent decay of the parts that touch the ground.

I. Cut an 8-foot 4 x 4 post to 5 feet and reuse the cut-off pieces to make the braces.

POST MOUNTING

Mounting a tiny structure on a post makes a lot of sense for the same reasons a mailbox is installed on a post: it's off the ground (where it won't get buried under snow or flooded with rain), it's easy to see, and it stays put. As mentioned, there are two basic methods for anchoring the structure to the post—wood or metal—and the choice largely comes down to aesthetics. A wood base has a traditional look and involves a bit more cutting and screwing. The metal base looks cleaner, but you have to buy the base in addition to the post. The method for anchoring the post in the ground is the same for both types.

BUILDING A WOOD POST BASE

This simple design uses a single 8-foot-long 4 × 4 post that you cut down to 5 feet, using the remaining post material for the two angled side braces. The only other wood is a 2 × 6 board that's as long as the side-to-side width of your structure. You can use PT lumber, cedar, or redwood for the post and board. Cedar and redwood will last longer if you use "heart" or "all heart" grade rather than standard grades. If you use PT lumber, make sure the post is rated for ground contact. Also, use HDG, stainless steel, or other screws specifically rated for PT lumber (see Fasteners and Hardware on page 26).

Cut the Post

Cut an 8-foot 4 × 4 post to length at 60 inches using a handsaw, circular saw, or power miter saw. To ensure a straight cut with a circular saw or handsaw, mark the cutting line along all four sides of the post using a rafter square or combination square. A circular saw can't cut all the way through a 4 × 4 in a single cut, so make one pass on one side, then flip the post over and cut from the opposite side. Set the 60-inch post aside for now.

Cut the Braces and Platform

Use a square to mark a 45-degree angle at one end of the 36-inch cut-off piece of post. Mark the angles on two opposing sides of the post, then mark straight lines connecting the angled lines. Cut the angle with a handsaw, circular saw, or power miter saw.

Measure from the angled end and mark the post at 10¾ inches. Starting at this mark, draw 45-degree cutting lines in the opposite direction from the first angle. Cut the piece at the marked angle. The resulting brace should measure 10¾ inches from point to point of the angled ends. Use the cut piece to trace the same angled lines onto the remaining leftover post material and make the cuts.

Measure the width along the bottom of your structure. Cut the 2 × 6 platform to fit the structure's base; it should be equal to or slightly smaller than the base. If the base is recessed (such as with a repurposed cabinet), the platform should fit inside the recess.

Install the Platform and Braces

Position the platform over the top end of the 60-inch post so it is centered side to side and front to back on the post. Fasten the platform to the post with two 3-inch deck screws or timber screws.

Position each brace under the platform so its angled faces are flush against the post and platform. Fasten each brace with two 3-inch screws driven into the platform and two into the post, driving each screw at an angle. When both braces are on, you're ready to install the post.

2. Trace along the ends of the cut brace to mark the second brace for cutting.

USING A METAL POST BASE

Metal post bases are designed for anchoring 4 × 4 wood fenceposts to concrete slabs or footings. In this application, the flat tabs, or flanges, of the base are anchored to the concrete and the post fits into the metal sleeve extending above the flanges. When used to anchor a tiny structure to a post, the base is turned upside down, and the flanges mount to the bottom of the structure.

Mounting the post base to the structure requires 1½-inch lag screws. This means the base material must be at least 1½ inches thick. If the structure is built with plywood, the base will likely be ⅝ inch or ¾ inch thick. To get to 1½ inches in thickness, you can add another layer or two of plywood to the base or install a 2 × 6 platform under the base, screwing through the base and into the platform with 1½-inch or 2-inch screws.

To mount the post base to the structure, center the base over the bottom of the structure or platform, making sure it is perfectly centered side to side and front to back. Drill a ⅛-inch pilot hole for each mounting hole in the base flanges. Anchor the post base to the structure with HDG ¼-inch × 1½-inch lag screws. Now you're ready to install the structure after the post is in place.

BURYING A WOOD POST

Before you do any digging in your yard (or anywhere else), call the national Call Before You Dig hotline at 8-1-1. This will trigger a notification to all utility companies (electrical, water, phone, and so on) with buried service lines in your area. They will send out

A posthole digger (also called a clamshell digger) makes a nice, round hole and allows you to stay upright (rather than repeatedly bending over) for most of the digging.

employees to mark the lines on your property. The whole process usually takes no more than three days, is completely free, and requires nothing more from you than a phone call. And that's why there's no excuse for digging somewhere you shouldn't and possibly damaging a utility line and/or hurting yourself (or worse).

While the utilities will take care of marking their underground lines, you are responsible for noting your own. It's easy to forget what's under your yard, so take the time to think of any systems you might have down there, such as:

- Sprinkler system tubing
- Landscape drains/French drains
- Wiring for landscape lights or outdoor outlets
- Electrical feeds to a shed or detached garage
- In-ground pet fencing

Dig the Posthole

Ready to dig? The best tools for the job are a posthole digger and a digging bar. The posthole digger lifts the dirt out of the hole, and the digging bar breaks up hard soil and rock. Most also have a tamper head on one end that's great for tamping soil around the post. If you don't have these specialty tools, you can use a narrow spade for digging and a 2 × 4 for tamping.

Dig the hole about 8 inches in diameter and at least 24 inches deep. If you're really feeling your oats, you can dig an extra 6 inches of depth and add a 6-inch layer of gravel to the bottom of the hole before putting in the post. This promotes drainage to slow the post's inevitable decay.

Anchor the Post

Set the post into the hole and begin backfilling around the post with the displaced soil. Tamp the first few inches of soil firmly around the post using the digging bar or a 2 × 4, then add some more soil and tamp again. When the post can stand up on its own, use a level to position it plumb (perfectly vertical). Hold the level on two adjacent sides of the post to check for plumb side to side and front to back.

Repeat this process of adding a few inches of soil, tamping, and checking for plumb until the hole is completely filled. Finally, overfill the hole slightly and create a tamped mound to help shed water away from the post. It's okay if grass or plants grow right around the post; you just want to avoid a depression that collects water, which would promote rot.

Check the post with a level frequently to make sure it stays plumb while you backfill and tamp.

Install Your Structure

If you built a wood platform, center the structure on top of the platform and secure it with six 2-inch deck screws driven through the structure bottom and into the platform. If you're using a metal post base, fit the structure and base onto the post and secure the base with eight ¼-inch × 2-inch HDG lag screws.

STRAIGHTENING A LEANING POST

Posts that lean to one side usually are caused by uneven settling or drainage of the surrounding soil, or possibly uneven tamping of the soil when the post was installed. The more you tamp soil, the more resistance it has to compressing. Areas that are tamped less thoroughly have more give and eventually let the post tilt in that direction.

The standard solution is to redo about half of the original installation: Dig out the soil around the post until you can straighten the post easily. Hold the post plumb (checking with a level) and repack the remaining soil in the hole (this time, use something really effective—like a digging bar—to get the soil as firm as possible). Then, backfill the hole a few inches at time, checking for plumb and tamping the soil thoroughly with each layer. Finish with a mound that sheds water away from the post.

With the structure sitting on top of the post, the assembly will be very top-heavy, so round up a helper or two to hold everything upright until the post is stable. Alternatively,

BELOW LEFT: Two sturdy shelf brackets offer an alternative for mounting smaller structures to their posts. **BELOW RIGHT:** Mount your structure to the post with deck screws (wood platform) or lag screws (metal post base).

Secure a post in problem soil with concrete. Use temporary braces (as seen at left) to hold the post plumb while the concrete cures.

you can temporarily brace the post with scrap boards and stakes. Drive the stakes into the ground, then attach a board to each with a single screw. Hold the post plumb and attach the other end of each board to the post with a screw.

It's also possible that your soil won't hold a post no matter how much you tamp it. Problem soils include clay soil on one end of the spectrum and very sandy soil on the other end. Clay soil holds onto water and becomes unstable and weak. Sandy soil drains well (unlike clay) but resists compaction (stays loose) and lacks weight and solid mass. If you think your soil is the real culprit, the best solution is to pull up the post, re-dig the hole, making it about 12 inches in diameter, and reset the post in concrete, using the same basic techniques used for a fencepost.

HANGING FROM TREES & FENCES

A tiny structure can be mounted to a tree or fence with screws driven through the back wall of the structure and into the tree or fencepost. For strength and longevity, it's a good idea to reinforce the back wall of the structure at each screw location. The reinforcement can be a strip

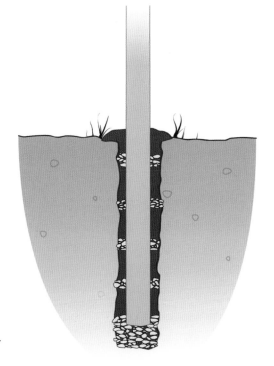

ROTTED POST

If you have to replace a post because it rotted after a few years, you probably used the wrong type of wood. Untreated pine (and similar softwoods) and standard grades of cedar and redwood don't last long when they're surrounded by earth. Your best bet is to use a PT post rated for ground contact. The only thing to do with a rotted post is to replace it. Trying to salvage the unrotted, aboveground portion of the post is more trouble than it's worth.

of lumber or plywood glued and screwed to the inside face of the back wall. Also, use a large washer under each screw head to prevent the head from digging into the wood.

MOUNTING TO A FENCEPOST

Use two or more timber screws or lag screws to mount a structure to a fencepost. Start by drilling oversize pilot holes through the back of the structure so the threads of the screws will slip through without grabbing the wood.

Clamp or screw a block of scrap wood to the fencepost to hold the structure's weight while you work. Set the structure into place against the post and check it with a level. Drill regular-size pilot holes into the post. (You can mount the structure on either side of the fence, but the screws should go into the center of a post for strength). Place a washer onto each screw and drive it into the post with a drill (for timber screws) or a ratchet wrench (for lag screws).

MOUNTING TO A TREE

Anchoring to a tree is different from mounting to a fencepost in that with a tree you should use only one big screw, as in a ½-inch-diameter lag screw. Here's why: Nutrients for a tree travel vertically via a layer just below the outer bark. If you drive one big screw through this layer and into the tree's solid wood, the tree can heal itself around the screw. But if you drive two screws (or any other fastener) close together in a vertical line, the tree material in between the screws can rot, creating a large wound. One big lag screw can easily hold a small structure, as long as it penetrates several inches into solid wood. It's also important not to remove the bark to create a flat spot for the structure. This would deprive the areas above and below the removed bark of nutrients, and expose the tree to infection and insects.

To anchor your structure to a tree, drill a ½-inch-diameter pilot hole (for a ½-inch lag screw) through the reinforced area of the structure's back wall; this is an oversize pilot hole that the lag will slip through. Drill a ⁵⁄₁₆-inch-diameter pilot hole in the tree, drilling only to the depth that the screw will penetrate. Add a large washer to the lag screw and drive it through the structure and into the tree with a ratchet wrench. It may help to start the lag by hitting it a couple of times with a hammer.

If the structure tilts forward or backward because the tree isn't plumb, you can shim behind it with a wedge or block of scrap wood. This is better for the tree than cutting off the bark.

FREESTANDING STRUCTURES

Freestanding structures stand on the ground or, more accurately, on a foundation on the ground. They shouldn't stand directly on the earth, because soil holds moisture, gets mushy, washes away, and generally isn't very stable. And moisture and instability aren't good for wood structures.

A foundation can be as simple as a few flat stones or concrete blocks or just a shallow bed of tamped gravel. If the area gets really wet during the rainy season, it might be a good idea to start with a gravel bed and place stones or blocks on top. The foundation should be flat and level, and it should keep the structure a bit higher than the surrounding ground, to promote drainage and to prevent water from pooling around the structure.

As for materials, stones can be any flat, wide specimens, such as flagstone or a block of cut stone. Concrete blocks can be solid patio stones or gray concrete blocks, which are sold in 2-inch and 4-inch thicknesses. Don't use standard cinder blocks with hollow cavities. Gravel can be anything that's relatively small and compacts well, such as bank run gravel, pea gravel, or crushed stone. Don't use river rock (which is roly-poly) or lava rock (which is very hard to work with).

To build a simple foundation with stones or blocks, remove all vegetation from the area, grade the soil flat, and tamp it with a hand tamper or with your feet. Place the stones or blocks on the soil and check them for level. Add soil or gravel under the stones or blocks to level them, as needed.

To build a gravel foundation, dig out 2 or 3 inches of soil and tamp the base with a hand tamper or your feet. The area should be a few inches larger than your structure. Fill the base with gravel, rake it smooth and flat, and tamp it. The top of the gravel should be an inch or so above the surrounding soil. Check the gravel with a level and add gravel and re-tamp as needed so the layer is flat and level.

A hand tamper is ideal for leveling and compacting gravel, but a pair of boots and some body weight work too.

LittleFreeLibrary.org®
Take a Book · Return a Book
Charter # 60879   A Nonprofit Organization

LITTLE FREE LIBRARY.org

JOIN US IN YOUR FRONT YARD AND
NEIGHBORHOODS WORLDWIDE.

SET UP A LIBRARY

DONATE

Learn more at
littlefreelibrary.org

Why Start a Little Free Library?

BY MARGRET ALDRICH, MEDIA + PROGRAMMING
MANAGER, LITTLE FREE LIBRARY

Building a Little Free Library book exchange and becoming a Little Free Library steward can enrich your life—and your community—in many ways.

Some people gravitate toward Little Free Libraries because they want to meet more neighbors and help bring their community together. Others want to increase book access for kids and adults in areas where books are scarce. And still others simply want to share the sheer joy of reading.

When you start your Little Free Library, you could spark all of these outcomes and more. Your "take a book, share a book" box may introduce a reluctant young reader to an author he or she loves, share a dose of kindness with a neighbor who needs it, or start a ripple effect of neighborhood engagement.

When you become a Little Free Library steward, you'll fit right in, because stewards come from all walks of life. Moms, dads, and grandparents often start their Little Free Libraries in their front yards to get kids excited about books. Teachers, principals, and school administrators echo this sentiment, bringing Little Free Libraries to schoolyards and playgrounds. Members of civic organizations work together to bring Little Free Libraries to well-loved parks and business fronts. Public librarians, both active and retired, are some of the most dedicated Little Free Library stewards. Even kids and teens can build, register, and steward their very own Little Free Libraries.

Your Little Free Library just might introduce a reluctant young reader to an author she or he loves.

Stewards not only come from all walks of life; they also come from all corners of the world. There are Little Free Libraries in every state, from California to New York and Alaska to Florida. You can find them in France, Italy, Japan, Brazil, Iceland, Russia, China, Ghana, Pakistan, India, and Australia. In fact, they're on every continent except Antarctica!

No matter where a Little Free Library is found, or who its caretaker is, those universal themes of community, care, and a love of books come back again and again.

Read on to hear straight from real-life stewards how having a Little Free Library can make a difference in your life and others' lives:

My first little library was a lovely gift from my father. This is my first home in Boston, and I wanted to build some community in this big and noisy city. On the first day that the library was up, I met three neighbors! My library is one way to make a big city feel like a small town.

BOSTON, MA

It took more than a year from the time I first heard of these libraries until ours was installed, but it was worth the wait! Almost every day (I'm checking!) a book is taken or a new book placed inside. The new connections with neighbors, the fun of putting a special

*book in the library to delight somebody, the newfound purpose behind book sale and
thrift-store browsing, the idea that parents are taking their kids past our library as part of
a new routine—all of this is a joy.*

ARROYO GRANDE, CA

*I am an immigrant who started from scratch in a country of many possibilities. After
twenty-one years I can do something for the neighbors and community. Even better
because I can get children to support and promote reading. We hope that no one will leave
empty-handed from the library.*

SCRANTON, PA

*The military sent us to the opposite coast one year ago. Our family hasn't had the easiest time
adjusting to our new home. West Coast versus East Coast is a big change in lifestyle! We feel
like misfits most the time. However, since installing our Little Free Library, we have now
met twice as many neighbors than we had in the past year. The Little Free Library really
does bring communities together. We have had such a sweet response from our neighborhood
utilizing the library and making a conversation starter among neighbors. Best gift ever!*

HAMPSTEAD, NC

**Little Free Libraries
can be found in all fifty
states, as well as in
several countries.
This library is located
in the Netherlands.**

*We discovered the first little library in Palo Alto and got inspired it to bring it to Milpitas.
I have two beautiful girls that love going from Little Free Library to Little Free Library and
pollinating them with new books. It's like a treasure hunt for
them. It's a great joy to see our neighbors pop by and check
out what is new at the Little Free Library. It's our little
contribution to our community.*

MILPITAS, CA

*My elderly neighbor with Parkinson's had been a recluse
as his disease progressed. When we opened our Little Free
Library, I passed out fliers inviting the neighborhood to join
us. We had twenty neighbors and five dogs, but by far our
most relished guest was John. He came up the street pulling
a wagon full of books to share! Everyone was delighted to see
him and he has once again become a part of the community!*

EL CAJON, CA

*[My favorite Little Free Library moment is thanks to] a boy
in our neighborhood who is dyslexic who uses our Little Free
Library to get books so he can choose a book at his reading
level without his friends seeing at school.*

CASTRO VALLEY, CA

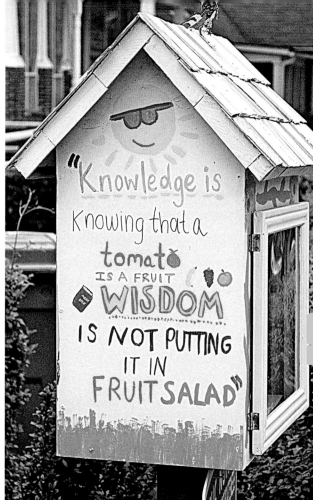

I never realized how much joy a little book house could bring to a neighborhood. I'm sitting here, on the sofa, watching the second family in the past thirty minutes visit the Little Free Library. I have a brain injury and spend most of my day confused and lost. Already, the Little Free Library has allowed me to focus and have a purpose every day.

MUSKEGON, MI

There have been so many happy little interactions with neighbors and community members because of this Little Free Library. But my favorite happened last summer when I was out weeding my garden. I was bent over, sweaty and dirty, when a happy and enthusiastic young girl came running up to me with a handful of books and her mother behind her, thanking me for the books. Then she asked me to come visit her Little Free Library on the south end of town. Little Free Libraries create community and create opportunities for the most lovely conversations and opportunities to share something of ourselves. They're a gift to the stewards and patrons both.

MOORHEAD, MN

Install your Little Free Library in a spot that is easily visible and accessible and has regular foot traffic—like this one near the sidewalk in front of a residence in Dearborn, Michigan.

GETTING THE WORD OUT ABOUT YOUR LIBRARY

You've followed all the steps of building a Little Free Library, from choosing your plans to painting or staining it. You've registered your Little Free Library with the national organization (see How to Register Your Library on page 156). Now, there's just one piece left: introduce it to your neighborhood!

This is your chance to celebrate your hard work and let your Little Free Library shine. Here are some tips on how to launch your friendly neighborhood book-sharing box.

Location, location, location. Where you place your Little Free Library will have a big effect on how successful it will be. Install your Little Free Library in a spot that is easily visible and accessible and has regular foot traffic. Near a sidewalk is ideal, so you'll often find Little Free Libraries in stewards' front yards. But anywhere where people gather works well: parks, schools, hospital waiting rooms, coffee shops, church lobbies, beaches, and more are good spots. (Note that you must get permission to place a Little Free Library on public grounds.)

Just add books. You'll need a small collection of books to fill your library before it launches. It's

Now just add books... and keep your Little Free Library well-stocked!

a good idea to start with a mix of books for a range of ages. (Though seasoned Little Free Library stewards will tell you that kids' books fly off the shelves first!) Have fun choosing your starter books—they could include favorites culled from your personal bookshelf, bestsellers picked up at a local used book store, or a hodgepodge of titles collected from friends and family for your Little Free Library's inaugural day. Leave room for others to drop off books too.

Host a grand opening. When you're ready to unveil your Little Free Library, throw a party to welcome it to the world! Your event can be as big or small as you're comfortable with. Invite your neighbors by dropping off simple fliers at their doors. (Find a sample flyer on the "Just for Stewards" page at www.littlefreelibrary.org.) If your neighborhood has a social media page or email list, send the invitation that way as well. Post notices at coffee shops and community bulletin boards and, the day of the event, set out signs or draw chalk messages on the sidewalk to invite people to stop by.

Your event could include a number of activities: a ribbon cutting for your Little Free Library, refreshments like lemonade and cookies, storytime for kids, a bookmark-making station, a table with coloring sheets and crayons, a "read to a dog" area (both dogs and kids seem to like this!), lawn games, music, and more. Decorate with balloons and banners to make it feel like a party and be sure to take lots of photos. Most importantly, have fun!

Invite the media. Let your local newspaper, TV stations, and radio stations know about your Little Free Library grand opening. The media is often looking for feel-good stories to share, and if your event is covered, it's a great way to tell your community about the Little Free Library and how it works. To contact local media, go to their websites to find their "news tips" lines or email addresses, then provide details about your Little Free Library event. You can find a sample press release on littlefreelibrary.org's "Just for Stewards" page.

Get on the map. Adding your Little Free Library to the online world map is another great way to spread the word about it. Go to www.littlefreelibrary.org/mapyourlibrary to upload your library's photo, location information, and story. When you add your Little Free Library to the map, you join a network of stewards all over the globe. This map is the most visited page on Little Free Library's website, with people using it to find Little Free Libraries near them, when at home or when traveling. Don't be surprised if your library gets a visitor from afar because he or she found you on the world map!

There are many strategies to keep neighbors coming back to your Little Free Library. If space permits, consider installing a place for book lovers to sit and visit or read.

ENCOURAGING COMMUNITY INVOLVEMENT

There aren't a lot of rules around having a Little Free Library book exchange. It can look like anything, from a log cabin to a medieval castle to a rocket ship, and it can hold any types of books you want to share. But there is one rule: Little Free Libraries belong to everyone and Little Free Libraries welcome everyone. That means you want the community to be as active and involved as possible! Here are a few of the best ways to engage your fellow residents.

Visitor information. When someone stumbles upon a Little Free Library for the first time, they may not know how it works. Leave a flier or notecard in your Library explaining the basics: visitors are free to take a book (even if they don't have one to share); they can return it later, pass it on, or keep it forever; or they can donate a book for someone else to discover.

Share stewardship duties. When your community understands that the Little Free Library is a neighborhood resource that benefits all, they in essence become your costewards. They can help keep the library tidy, thriving, and full of books. Ask friends and neighbors to help keep an eye on your Little Free

Library, especially when you'll be out of town. Enlist them to spread the word about the Little Free Library, keep it neat, and gather books if your inventory runs low.

Host a book party. Even if you've already had an initial grand opening, there are other reasons to celebrate with your Little Free Library patrons. Maybe you want to serve cupcakes on your Little Free Library's first birthday. Maybe you want to kick off a summer of reading with a last-day-of-school party. Or maybe you want to whoop it up on your favorite author's birthday.

Add a guest book. When you keep a guest book and pen in your Little Free Library, you might be surprised by the heartfelt thank-you notes and other missives you receive from members of the community. A word of caution: guest books can sometimes walk away with a visitor by accident, so don't use anything that you'd be upset to lose. Some stewards use real journals, while others make DIY guest books from index cards.

Start an Action Book Club. The Action Book Club, an initiative of the Little Free Library organization, combines reading with community service—think of it as "good reads and good deeds." Great for any age group, an Action Book Club reads and discusses a book, then works together to do something positive for the neighborhood. Check out littlefreelibrary.org/actionbookclub to learn more and sign up with people from your community.

Get creative. What other kinds of activities would your Little Free Library patrons love? Perhaps you could organize a Little Free Library crawl, during which a group bikes, walks, or drives to visit local Little Free Libraries. Maybe you could host a Little Free Library design contest, in which participants draw their dream library to enter to win a small prize. Or maybe you post new book trivia in your Little Free Library each week for visitors to find.

Help a neighborhood in need. Do you know of a nearby location that would benefit from a Little Free Library full of books? Work with your community to bring a Little Free Library book exchange to that area and keep it stocked with good-quality books. Not only can you pay it forward with your own Little Free Library; you can encourage and help others to become part of the Little Free Library movement.

TIPS FOR A LIVELY COLLECTION

When everything is running smoothly, your Little Free Library should be a self-sustaining system, with books coming and going in equal measure, thanks to the generosity of friends and visitors. Here are our top ideas for keeping your Little Free Library book inventory at its best.

Mix it up. Try to stock books for many different age groups and for many different tastes. Including fiction, nonfiction, board books, young-adult novels, comic books, cookbooks, and more will ensure that nearly everybody who opens your Little Free Library door will find something to get excited about. Remember to stock diverse books too, so all the people in your community can see themselves reflected in the pages.

Celebrate special days. Stewards often enjoy highlighting authors, holidays, and more in their Little Free Libraries—from paying homage to Harry Potter to celebrating Black History Month. Some stewards even have a scary-book theme for Halloween or a gardening theme when spring arrives.

Keep up the quality. Although it's important to have a mix of books, make sure that those books are of good quality. If you receive old, musty paperbacks with the covers falling off, it's okay to pull them out of your library and recycle them. Really! A good rule of thumb is this: would I lend this book to a friend of mine? If not, it may need to be retired.

Getting more books. If your Little Free Library's book inventory is getting low, there are lots of ways to fill it up again. The simplest way is to ask your library visitors! Let them know with a friendly sign on your library that books are needed. Friends, family, and coworkers can be good sources of books, and so are public library book sales, thrift stores, and used book shops. Visit www.littlefreelibrary.org/books for access to low-cost books and special book giveaways.

Finally, don't forget to register your Little Free Library. Each officially registered Little Free Library book exchange is given a unique charter number.

HOW TO REGISTER YOUR LIBRARY

Don't forget to register your library with the Little Free Library nonprofit organization. Each official, registered Little Free Library book exchange is given a unique charter number that grants you membership perks and makes you part of the Little Free Library Sharing Network family.

Insider tip: You can register your Little Free Library before it's complete, so your charter sign will arrive while the library is still under construction.

Your registration brings numerous benefits, including:

- An official charter sign engraved with your library's charter number.
- The option to add your Little Free Library to the world map. People will use the map to find and visit your library.
- Access to a private Facebook group for registered stewards. Swap stories, ask questions, and connect with other stewards near and far.
- A steward's guidebook of proven tips to make your library a vital part of your community.
- A "How Does This Library Work?" flier for your library.
- A subscription to a regular e-newsletter with inspiring stories, ideas, and deals.
- Access to brand-new, deeply discounted books.
- Surprise book giveaways and contests from Little Free Library and the nonprofit's publishing partners, only for registered stewards.

Once your Little Free Library is registered, the charter sign is attached, and the library is open for business, snap some photos and add your location to the Little Free Library world map. While you're there, enjoy perusing photos and stories from other Little Free Library stewards around your area, around the United States, and around the globe—all of whom care about literacy and community, just like you!

To register your library and put it on the map, go to www.littlefreelibrary.org/registration-process.

A painted finish not only adds an element of interest, which in turn attracts visitors and perhaps even sparks discussion—done right, it also can help protect your structure from harmful elements. If you opt for paint over stain, as these owners have done, be sure to go with a 100-percent acrylic exterior paint. Just keep in mind that the structure will require periodic touchup and recoating.

Some owners opt for a more rustic, unpainted look. In such cases, it's still a good idea to protect your structure with an outdoor clearcoat to help block harmful UV rays that break down wood over time. These Little Free Libraries are both located in northern Minnesota. The steeply peaked log cabin structure is located at Mesaba Co-op Park. The builder repurposed wood and household items, such as rulers for the window frames and even an old fuse for the doorknob. If you choose to upcycle wood, be sure it's free of lead-based paints—your neighborhood hardware store or home center sells inexpensive test kits.

Interested in establishing a Little Free Library in front of your home, or maybe in a community space? The good news is you have many options when it comes to your structure, including assembling a ready-to-build kit from Little Free Library or building from a plan and then registering the completed structure. That's only the beginning—your options for finishing and kitting out your structure are limited mostly by your imagination.

RIGHT AND BELOW: The roof's job is to take one for the team (i.e., absorb most of the punishment doled out by sun, snow, and rain). There are a number of options when it comes to roofing. The white library shown here has asphalt shingles of the sort found on most residential houses in the US. You can opt to step up the design a bit by using an attractive cedar lap siding finished with an oil stain to help delay drying. A third option, as seen in a few plans in this book, is aluminum or galvanized sheet metal.

ABOVE AND FOLLOWING PAGES: Use architectural interest to complement the predominant architecture of life-size dwellings in your area, or just to attract curiosity. The builders of the two-doored Little Free Library, located in Apex, North Carolina, created a white picket fence and scale-size cedar shakes for the roof. Similarly, the white structure features scaled clapboard siding, mimicking a common detail of nineteenth-century American architecture. Even details as simple as a side trim and an inexpensive rosette painted a complementary color can add charm to a structure.

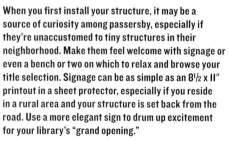

When you first install your structure, it may be a source of curiosity among passersby, especially if they're unaccustomed to tiny structures in their neighborhood. Make them feel welcome with signage or even a bench or two on which to relax and browse your title selection. Signage can be as simple as an 8½ x 11" printout in a sheet protector, especially if you reside in a rural area and your structure is set back from the road. Use a more elegant sign to drum up excitement for your library's "grand opening."

TOP RIGHT AND ABOVE: Your climate is an obvious consideration when building and finishing your tiny structure. The structure's primary job is to keep its contents safe and dry. When it comes to snowy areas, the best designs have overlap-style or snugly fitting inset doors, a good roof overhang, and an installation that places the structure above the likely deepest snowfall. In most areas 3 feet is sufficient. **TOP LEFT AND MIDDLE:** These libraries, located on a Massachusetts beach and the Florida Keys, must withstand elements of another nature. **LEFT:** Your structure will eventually take a beating from the elements wherever you live. It's important to stay on top of maintenance. Once wood is exposed to water and UV light for more than a season, it's difficult to recover and more expensive and time-consuming replacement may be your only option.

Rather than build a new structure from a kit or plans, some owners opt to upcycle found or discarded items. The result is both unique and efficient. These not-tiny telephone-booths-turned-libraries are in the United Kingdom. The brown former display case was spotted on a street in Dusseldorf, Germany. Whenever you upcycle, be sure to check that the materials used on the structure are free of harmful features like sharp edges and lead paint.

Beginning with Todd Bol's tiny schoolhouse library in Hudson, Wisconsin, **Little Free Library** has inspired tens of thousands of sharing exchanges around the world, such as these boxes in **Spain** and **Poland**. Today you can find registered Little Free Libraries in every state and on every continent except Antarctica!